Webify Your Business

Internet Marketing Secrets for the Self-Employed

Patrick Schwerdtfeger

The ultimate step-by-step guide for small business owners, commission salespeople and service professionals.

Published by Lulu.

ISBN: 978-0-557-04901-1

Corporate Wholesale Quantities & Pricing

100 –	249	copies	$ 15.00 ea.
250 –	499	copies	14.00
500 –	999	copies	13.00
1,000 –	2,499	copies	12.00
2,500 –	4,999	copies	10.00
5,000 –	9,999	copies	8.00 *
10,000 +		copies	6.00 *

* *Includes a half-day onsite workshop with Patrick Schwerdtfeger.
Travel expenses will be billed separately.*

*www.**tactical**execution.com*

This book is dedicated to the

44th President of the United States.

You inspire so many.

Acknowledgements

I would like to take this opportunity to thank those who have inspired me from afar. Each in their own way, they exhibit the qualities I value and the strategies I espouse.

Barack Obama, you personify the American Dream. You are using the strategies laid out in this book better than anyone before you. I have never been more proud to be an American.

Seth Godin, you see the future. Although I didn't know your name as I wrote my first book, the concepts in *"Make Yourself Useful, Marketing in the 21st Century"* closely resemble those in *"Permission Marketing."*

Michael Krasny, your intellect is amazing. I have enjoyed your program for years and hope to one day express my own thoughts with the same lyrical eloquence you exhibit every morning in your Forum program.

John Reese, you are a pioneer. I have followed you since the early days and always take notice when your name pops up in my email inbox. You were the first one who inspired me to hone my craft.

Frank Kern, you epitomize internet success. Your authentic and casual approach is refreshing. Thank you for the email subject lines that tantalize my curiosity and the videos that beg for action.

You are my heroes. Thank you. I am grateful to live alongside you during this changing and exciting time.

Foreword

Buy this book for your distributors, commission salespeople or independent brokers, giving them:

☐ Internet marketing information they *want* and *need*.
☐ Practical and unthreatening step-by-step instructions.
☐ Short accessible chapters they can read in 10 minutes.
☐ Itemized to-do lists at the end of each chapter.
☐ A perfect format for both beginner & savvy recipients.

Corporate wholesale volume discounts are listed at the very beginning of this book.

Webify **Your Business** is specifically designed for small business owners, commission salespeople and self-employed service professionals. It offers highly practical step-by-step instructions on how they can leverage the internet to build their businesses.

These people *need* this information. They *want* this information. They are ready to act!

Today's economy is difficult. Budgets are tight. This book represents an ideal and inexpensive gift for your busy sales force; a gift that will help them sell more of your product.

Volume orders are printed with a blank space on the back cover where you can brand the book with your company name, logo and full contact information.

Patrick Schwerdtfeger is available for keynote speeches as well as onsite half-day and full-day workshops. Contact us for rates and scheduling details.

www.tacticalexecution.com

Table of Contents

Calibrate Your Online Identity

Drive Traffic to Your Website

Conclusions and Execution

1

Introduction

Are you ready? Are you ready to start building your online identity? Are you ready to embrace the technology and work your way up the learning curve? Are you ready to reclaim your business and find your future clients on the internet?

If so, you're in the right place. This book is specifically designed for aspiring entrepreneurs, small business owners, commission salespeople and service professionals. Not only will it introduce you to all the latest internet marketing techniques, but it will walk you by the hand, step by step, through the process.

This book tells you how to get things done. You'll notice the contents are split into 60 individual chapters, each with a narrow and specific focus. You can read a chapter in 10 minutes or less and get immediate tactical guidance on the strategy and the process.

Each chapter (except for this one) concludes with an itemized to-do list, allowing you to break the topic into specific tasks to make progress and see results quickly.

I have also put a lot of attention into the *order* of these chapters. You can waste an enormous amount of time doing things in the wrong order. More than half the value in this book is the step-by-step presentation.

Regardless where your business is today, follow along with the steps laid out in this book. Together, we can build your online identity from the ground up. This book is designed to make the online opportunity available and accessible to anyone who's willing to do the work.

Here's the sad reality …

Most people don't *do* anything. Most people never take action. They say they will but they don't. They get excited but it fades. As a result, most people never see real results and eventually get discouraged and give up.

I can give you the best advice in the world, but it won't do anything unless you take action. I've done the research and this book offers incredible guidance and powerful tools but the actual implementation is up to you.

Please commit to this process. Create a folder and track your progress. Go through the steps and embrace curiosity when confronting the unfamiliar. The strategies presented in this book are here because they produce results.

Together, we'll build a strategic foundation for your business that's far more sophisticated than most businesses ever achieve. Together, we'll take steps that will leave your business far better positioned than it is today.

Before we get started, please visit the Tactical Execution website and take advantage of all the free resources I have there. You'll find educational videos, audio interviews with experts, dozens of articles, hundreds of useful links, text versions of all my podcasts and PDF downloads, all designed to help you grow your business.

Tactical Execution > Resources

The first section of this book is devoted to defining your business model. This may seem unrelated to internet marketing but nothing could be further from the truth. A clear and focused business model is essential to effective internet positioning.

Everybody uses the internet differently. We all have our own favorite platforms and our own way of accessing information. But the one thing that remains constant for all of us is the mechanism of finding information online.

Search engines and social media platforms are rewarding websites that offer extensive but focused information about their topic. The websites that shine are those that present a clear purpose with easily understood benefits and a *landslide* of good information. These websites can only be built by companies who have a well-defined business focus.

Work through these first few chapters and do the exercises suggested. They will force you to hone your business model and fine-tune your value proposition. That clarity adds to your business foundation and pays dividends online and off.

Tell your friends about this book! People can purchase it or sign-up for the free email course at the following website:

> http://www.WebifyBook.com/

If you'd like to join a local **Web**ify **Business Club** (or start your own – see Chapter 20 & 58), visit the following:

> http://www.WebifyClub.com/

The Twitter hashtag (explained in Chapter 31) for this book is #webify. Please include it in all related tweets.

Let's get started!

2

Develop Expertise

Are you an expert? ... well? ... are you??

The answer is YES. Yes, you are. You're an expert. Get used to it!

On what? I don't know. You need to figure that out.

Permission Marketing (the title of a brilliant book written by Seth Godin) is all about being an expert. It's all about providing value. It's all about building trust.

"Make Yourself Useful; Marketing in the 21st Century"

That's the title of my first book and it's all about the exact same concept. In today's information society, you need to carve out a little slice of the universe and claim it as your own. You need to decide what your specialty is and become an expert in that field.

A common phrase in internet marketing circles is "go an inch wide and a mile deep." Search engines like Google love narrow little niches that people exploit with huge expertise. Chris Anderson describes this as "the long tail."

It's the same idea. Pick a specific topic and become an expert in that field.

This involves three steps:
1. Pick a narrow specific topic.
2. Acquire massive expertise.
3. Present yourself as an expert.

I'll leave step one to you. And we'll be dealing with step three in the next chapter. But step two is tactical. Step two is structural. Step two we can work with.

Set some time aside and do an exercise that will blow your mind! Pick a few keywords to describe your specialty and do the following:

Go to EzineArticles.com and do a search for those keywords. You'll find thousands of free articles other people have written about your topic.

Go to the iTunes Music Store, click on Podcasts, then Power Search and do a search for your keywords. You'll find hundreds of free audio podcasts about your topic. Sort the results by popularity and subscribe to the top ones. Listen to them while commuting to work or getting some exercise at the gym.

Go to YouTube and do a search for your keywords. You'll find incredible free videos people have made about your topic. Watch them and learn. Not only will you be introduced to your competition but you'll gain tremendous expertise in the process.

This exercise demonstrates the unbelievable resources at your finger tips. It also helps you refine your specialty. You'll see what others are already doing and what they're *not* doing, at least not yet.

Pick your topic. Stake your claim. Figure out what you're an expert in.

I have a whole CD devoted entirely to this process. It's called "Recognized Expert" and you can find it on the Tactical Execution website.

Tactical Execution > Store > Marketing Products

Step-by-step action guide:

- ☐ *Decide on a field you can specialize in.*
- ☐ *Select a few keywords for your specialty.*
- ☐ *Use them to find articles on Ezine Articles.*
- ☐ *Use them to find podcasts on iTunes.*
- ☐ *Use them to find videos on YouTube.*
- ☐ *Make notes and build your expertise.*
- ☐ *Notice what your competition is doing.*
- ☐ *Notice what your competition is **not** doing.*

Develop Expertise

3

Limiting Beliefs

When it comes to growing your business, one of the most important things you can do is get your belief systems in check. People often become their own worst enemy.

They don't do it intentionally. They may not even realize they're doing it. But in many cases, they do. Why? It's their limiting beliefs. Whether you realize it or not, your belief systems define almost everything you do.

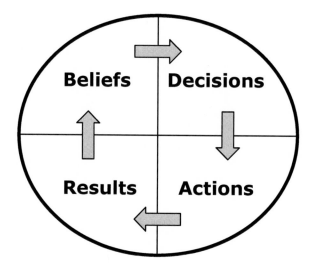

Consider the diagram on the previous page. Your Beliefs form the foundation of your Decisions. Your Decisions lead to your Actions. Your Actions define your Results. And your Results feed back into your Beliefs.

On May 6, 1954, Roger Bannister broke the four-minute mile for the first time in human history. It had never been done before. Many doctors even believed the human heart was incapable of enduring such an incredible strain. They were wrong.

But ...

Bannister's record was broken just 46 days later. During the next three years, 16 athletes had achieved the same thing and hundreds more have broken the four-minute mile since then. As of this writing, the current record is three minutes and 43 seconds.

What changed? The belief system.

Up until that day, nobody believed it was possible. Once someone proved that it *was* possible, the belief system changed. After that, the mental barrier was gone and the new results reflected the new beliefs.

You need to work on your own belief systems. Even if you're already successful, I'm willing to bet there's still a gap between where you *are* and where you'd like to *be*. Different people advocate different approaches.

Law of Attraction programs start in the Beliefs quadrant. By imagining and focusing on what you want, you can trick your mind into a different belief system and that can roll through the circle and improve your results.

A lot of motivational speakers start in the Decisions quadrant. By making a single decision - a decision to take action - you can change your life forever. Anthony Robbins comes to mind, and the statement is true. One decision *can* change everything.

Some even start in the Results quadrant. By pretending like you're already there - and living like it - you can get some traction and start a domino affect that improves the level of your performance (but that's a risky approach).

Tactical Execution focuses on the Actions quadrant. We focus on the specific tactics that get results. If you know which actions deliver results, changing your beliefs is easy.

But regardless of the approach, you need to start a deliberate program to ensure you actually *believe* you're an expert. If you don't, you'll end up sabotaging your own efforts and making it harder to achieve the goals you've set for yourself.

Believing in yourself is easier said than done. Confidence grows out of an established pattern of success. This book is designed precisely for that purpose. Small steps and small victories add up quickly.

Step-by-step action guide:

- ☐ *Take ownership of your own expertise.*
- ☐ *Select which quadrant you'll focus on first.*
- ☐ *If it's Beliefs, start visualizing your success.*
- ☐ *If it's Decisions, make that decision today.*
- ☐ *If it's Actions, start mapping out your plan.*
- ☐ *If it's Results, be careful – this is risky.*
- ☐ *Focus only on your desired destination.*
- ☐ *Establish a pattern of success.*

Limiting Beliefs

4

Problems + PAIN = Profit

I was recently introduced to a brilliant little equation by Christine Comaford, one of the original angel investors for Google. And it's so true ...

Problems + PAIN = Profit

There are two basic requirements for a successful business model. Many businesses have only one. Many more have none at all! If you want to build your business, you need to make absolutely sure that you have *both*.

First, you need a problem that you can solve. There needs to be something *wrong*. Take a look at your area of expertise and ask yourself where the problems are.

What's missing? What doesn't work properly? What are people always struggling with? Write down your answers.

Second, people need to be in *pain* because of the problem. This is important. There are lots of problems that nobody cares about. They don't result in *pain*. And because of that, people won't be willing to spend their hard-earned money to fix them.

You need to find the people who are in pain. Who is suffering? *That's* your target market. That's your audience. That's your ideal customer. That's who is looking for *you* and is ready to spend money on your product.

I know this stuff may sound trivial but let me tell you; most companies never go through this basic exercise. If you get a clear picture of exactly what problem you solve and what *pain* you alleviate, everything you do going forward will be more efficient and more effective.

I've created a worksheet to walk you through this step and you can find it (in PDF format) on my website. It's called "Define the Need Worksheet".

Tactical Execution > Resources > Downloads

Set some time aside – maybe 30 minutes or an hour – to ask yourself these questions. Put your work into your Tactical Execution file. We'll be coming back to it in the next chapter and taking the next step.

Step-by-step action guide:

 Identify the problem your product solves.
Describe the pain caused by the problem.
Note the emotional distress you alleviate.
Focus marketing on emotional benefits.

Problems + PAIN = Profit

5

Value Proposition

So ... what do you sell?

In the last chapter, we isolated the problem your product or service addresses. More importantly, we identified the *pain* caused by the problem. The people who experience that pain are your target market. They're the ones who are ready to spend money on your product or service.

The next step is to identify and understand exactly what your product is. What do you sell? Specifically. Is it a silly question? Let's take a closer look.

Does Starbucks sell coffee? I would say NO. Starbucks sells an environment, an experience. When MacDonald's introduced a variety of high-end coffees, were they really competing with Starbucks? No, they weren't. In fact, they didn't even pretend to compete.

MacDonald's sells a few high-end coffees. Starbucks sells an experience. Two different things. They appeal to two entirely different audiences. To that end, MacDonald's specifically addressed the unpretentiousness of their specialty coffees in their advertising campaign.

If you really want to grow your business, you need to focus on the people, not the product. You don't sell your product's features. You sell your product's benefits. Even better; you sell the emotions your customers experience when they *use* your product.

Think back to our discussion about *pain* in the last chapter. What you're selling is the alleviation of that pain. You're selling the emotions your customers experience when the pain is finally gone.

In the case of Starbucks, they're selling a feeling of comfort; a tiny little vacation people go on every time they step into a Starbucks store. Their customers escape their lives, even if just for a moment. They take time to breathe. They leave the craziness behind and take a short vacation with their Starbucks coffee.

Think about the emotions *your* product delivers. You'll need to get it done before the next chapter because we'll be working on your 30-second Elevator Pitch and you *need* to know what you sell before then. Get a pen and paper. Jot down some notes. And figure out exactly what you sell.

Step-by-step action guide:

- ☐ *List all your product (or service) features.*
- ☐ *Identify a benefit for each feature.*
- ☐ *Describe an emotion for each benefit.*
- ☐ *Define your business in terms of emotions.*
- ☐ *Focus your marketing on those emotions.*

Value Proposition

6

Elevator Pitch

Let's start with a definition. An "Elevator Pitch" is a really concise way of describing what your company does. It's usually 90 words or less and was given its name because you should be able to tell someone exactly what you do while you're on an elevator together – about 30 seconds.

So ... what's yours? What's your Elevator Pitch?

Fact is; the vast majority of companies don't have this simple but essential positioning statement in place. They never took the time to put it into words. They never took the time to define their business model in clear concise language.

We're going to change that.

Your Elevator Pitch is a metaphorical equivalent to your business focus. Most businesses don't have a true focus. Taking the time to write an effective Elevator Pitch forces you to find your focus. Your Elevator Pitch forms the foundation for your entire business and, in particular, all of your online marketing efforts.

Before we start crafting your pitch and identifying your focus, we need to define the objective. What are we actually trying to accomplish? This is important! We want people to *know* what you sell, *want* what you sell and *buy* what you sell – in just 30 seconds.

In order to do that, we need to use every second wisely. We need a strategy. We need every word to play a role. So here's what to do. Write your Elevator Pitch one sentence at a time. There are four in all.

Sentence #1 needs to identify who you are. Start by taking the following format: hello, my name is XXX and I am a(n) YYY specializing in ZZZ. I know it's simple but it's a start. You can refine it later.

Sentence #2 needs to describe your specialty in more detail. But it needs to do more than that. It also needs to identify the problem that exists and how you solve that problem. Here's where we bring in the *pain* we identified in Chapter 4. Try to work that in somehow. Identify the problem and explain how your product alleviates the *pain* caused by the problem.

Sentence #3 needs to differentiate you from your competition. Why are you better? What makes you different? You need to use this sentence to establish credibility, build value and provide proof. If you have statistics to back up your claim, include them. If other products are more expensive, say so. If you deliver better results, make that clear.

And finally, **sentence #4** needs to give a call-to-action. Tell them what to do next. Be specific. What action do you want them to take? Say it! This is often the most difficult part but it's also the most important. Tell them what to do. People like direction and hate surprises. Be confident and be honest. Tell them what to do next.

Now, put it all together. Write it all in paragraph format and read it to yourself. Make adjustments and try different words. When you're happy with it, read it to your friends and work colleagues. Read it to people who have no idea what you do and ask them if your four-sentence Elevator Pitch makes it clear.

Here are a couple last-minute tips. First, don't say too much. Make sure your pitch is 90 words or less. It needs to be precise and quick – no run-on sentences. Clear simple statements. That's it.

Second, dumb it down. Seriously. Get rid of the jargon, even the ones you think everybody should know. They don't. People who are not in your field don't know those 'easy' words. So take them out. Your pitch needs to be written at a 6th grade level. Simple, simple. You want an 11-year-old child to hear your pitch and understand what you do.

This project is far more important than you might think. It forms the basis for everything else you do. In the next chapter, we'll start defining your target market. Once you know exactly what you do and you also know where your target market is, we're in business!

Step-by-step action guide:

☐ *Allocate time to write your Elevator Pitch.*
☐ *Sentence #1: Identify yourself.*
☐ *Sentence #2: What problem do you solve?*
☐ *Sentence #3: Why are you better?*
☐ *Sentence #4: Give a call-to-action!!*
☐ *Made adjustments and refine it over time.*

Elevator Pitch

7

Target Market

Where are your customers?

No business can succeed without them! If you're in the process of starting or growing your business, it can't hurt to set some time aside and really try to understand your audience.

Before we begin, let's review the past three chapters. First, we identified the problem your product solves. But more importantly, we looked at the *pain* some people feel as a result of that problem. It's those people who are ready to spend money.

After that, we looked at the business model in slightly more philosophical terms. What exactly do you sell? This step is important because a lot of businesses think they sell features. They don't. They sell benefits. But going a step further, they actually sell the emotional feeling people experience when they use the product.

When marketing your product, don't communicate the features, at least not right at the beginning. Don't even focus on the benefits. That's not the most important thing.

Tell them about the emotional feeling! That's what will motivate them to buy.

In Chapter 6, we pulled it together and crafted a 30-second Elevator Pitch. This four-sentence pitch identifies who you are, what the problem is, how you solve it, what makes you different and what people should do to get started.

Now, let's look at a few tools you can use to find your target market. Whether you want to market your product online or offline, the internet provides some great resources to help you understand your customers. Start by visiting the free Google keyword selector tool. You can find the link on the Tactical Execution website.

Tactical Execution > Resources > Useful Links > Keyword Research Links

Once at the Google tool, you can enter a few keywords that relate to your product and quickly get a long list of related words and phrases. Sort the results by Average Volume and you can immediately see what people are searching for most often in your area of expertise.

This simple little technique is incredibly powerful. Within seconds you can see exactly what people are searching for and it will also give you some insight as to where you might find those people.

This type of visibility was never possible before. In the offline world, you had to do focus groups or surveys to understand what your market was thinking. No longer. Today, you can visit this free tool any time you like and get direct access to the exact preferences of the population.

You can also visit http://directory.big-boards.com/ and search for the same keywords. You'll quickly find forums and discussion boards where people are talking about your topic. Conversations are markets on today's social internet. We'll talk about that more in Chapter 28. If you want to access a market, participate in the conversation.

One of the biggest forums on the internet is Yahoo Answers. Once logged in, you can either ask a question or provide an answer to someone else' question. This is a spectacular place to touch your audience. If you answer questions you know answers to, your contribution will be viewed by precisely those people looking for that information. We'll go into more detail in Chapter 53.

This is one of the best things about the internet. On almost any interactive website, you can isolate your target market with unparalleled precision by simply demonstrating your own expertise in the public domain. The only people who will find your contribution are those people who are looking precisely for that information.

I also recommend putting your keywords into a Google search and seeing what comes up. Whatever shows up is what your customers are finding. Look at the organic results in the center of the page. Those are your biggest online competitors. Look on the right hand column of "sponsored links". That's what other people are trying to sell your audience.

Think about what your customers have in common. What are their interests? What's their profession? What other activities do they participate in? The more you know about your audience, the more ideas you'll have for finding them.

Sometimes your first instinct isn't the best choice. As an internet marketing consultant, for example, a forum about internet marketing isn't my market. It's my competition.

Instead, a forum for small business owners or financial advisors or real estate agents is much better. Those are the people who need my expertise. The people on the internet marketing forum already have it – at least they think they do!

Look for groups on Facebook (Chapter 29) or LinkedIn (Chapter 30). Look for clubs on Meetup or Yahoo Groups

(Chapter 58). Search for the top bloggers on Technorati (Chapter 25). All of these activities help you isolate your target market.

Start compiling a list of all the places where you find people interested in your field. Once we get into the later sections of this book, this list will determine where you spend your time.

Step-by-step action guide:

☐ *Visit the free Google Keyword Tool.*
☐ *Learn what your market is searching for.*
☐ *Visit the Big-Boards forum directory.*
☐ *Find the biggest online forums in your field.*
☐ *Put your keywords into a Google search.*
☐ *See who your biggest competitors are.*
☐ *Read the "sponsored links" on Google.*
☐ *Search for groups on Facebook & LinkedIn.*
☐ *Search clubs on Meetup & Yahoo Groups.*
☐ *Search top bloggers on Technorati.com.*
☐ *Make note of the good potential markets.*

Target Market

8

List of Prospects

Now that your business is almost ready to launch, who will you call first?

You would be amazed how many businesses try to launch before they have assembled a list of potential prospects. Don't waste precious time and money attempting to get sales without building a list first.

If your customers are all in a single profession, your job is fairly easy. For example, let's say you plan to sell your product to dentists or auto mechanics or lawyers. You can quickly go to switchboard.com or yellowpages.com and do a search for those keywords.

These websites then offer you a list of categories to refine your search. By selecting a particular category and entering a ZIP code, you can immediately get a list of all your prospects in that area.

Of course, the list will probably span multiple pages with only 10 listings on each. But with a little patience along with the copy & paste functions on your computer, you can transfer all that information into an Excel spreadsheet in an hour or two. In Excel, you can manipulate the data and organize it into different columns or categories. Is it a menial job? Sure. But the list is invaluable.

I did this back in 2002. I was compiling a list of Escrow Officers for my notary business and used <u>switchboard.com</u> to do so. In less than two hours, I had a list of 200 local escrow offices in an Excel file with columns for company name, street address, city name, state, zip code, phone number and fax number. Done.

Here's another golden secret. You may be familiar with a company called InfoUSA. They maintain an enormous database and sell lists to paying customers. As it turns out, you can go to your public library and access a database called ReferenceUSA, a sister company to InfoUSA but one that is paid for by the government.

What does that mean? It means you can get the exact same data as InfoUSA for free. The only downside is that you are usually restricted to the number of listings you can download in one sitting. Other than that, it's exactly the same.

ReferenceUSA is an incredibly powerful resource and it doesn't cost a penny. It's one of the best kept secrets I'm aware of. Take advantage of it. Schedule an hour to visit your local library and ask the person at the Reference Desk to show you how to access and use it.

In many cases, you can access from your home computer with a library card number and your last name. Once logged in, you can sort on a variety of different criteria and quickly put a list together that will let you and your business hit the ground running.

Lastly, do a few Google searches for your keywords and the word "directory". Most industries have public online directories. When I first opened Box14 Financial, a company that liquidated seller financing business notes, I compiled a list of over 5500 Business Brokers across the country. It only took about four hours, all because I found two online directories and was able to copy and paste the entire list to my own computer.

Growing your business is a lot easier when you have a list of prospects. It's a tedious job but you only have to do it once. Set some time aside to do the research. When it's all done, you'll be happy you did.

Step-by-step action guide:

- ☐ *Search your keywords on <u>switchboard.com</u>.*
- ☐ *Search ReferenceUSA at your local library.*
- ☐ *Google for your keywords plus "directory".*
- ☐ *Copy and paste the information into Excel.*
- ☐ *Organize the data into a series of columns.*
- ☐ *Import into a contact management system.*

List of Prospects

9

Email Distribution Lists

Email is powerful. Why? Because you can click Send and have your message reach thousands of people in an instant, and it won't cost you a penny.

There are basically three different ways to market your product or service by email.
1. Email to your own list.
2. Email to a Joint Venture list.
3. Email to a Distribution List.

Emailing to your own list is just that. You send out a message to a list of email addresses you've accumulated on your own. There are some great strategies for doing that and we'll go over them in more detail in Chapter 19, after we've covered a few website topics.

Joint Ventures. What's that? It's when you approach someone else in your field who already has a big email list and then send a message out to *their* list for a split of the resulting revenue. It's an incredibly powerful way of getting your products in front of a huge audience quickly.

But it's not always that easy.

It's very common for good Joint Venture (JV) partners to require a substantial split of the revenue. If you're selling information products (like how-to PDF documents, for example), the split can be as high as 50% or 75%. Furthermore, you'll never see their list. You just give them the text you want to send and they'll do the rest.

Let's break down the strategy. You're not getting their list. You're just "renting" it. But if someone buys your product, you obviously get all their contact information at that point. So the idea is to do JV deals with an irresistible offer, generating a big response. That way, you're building your own list with all the people who accept the offer.

There's always a bit of a balancing act because the list owner wants to make money on the deal. That means he or she probably won't be very happy if you basically just offer something for free. In fact, he or she probably won't allow it at all.

Usually, people offer a "front end" product – something cheap with impressive value – and a "back end" product that costs more money. The initial email promotes the front end product and those who purchase it are offered an up-sell for the (usually more expensive) back end product.

The list owner usually makes a higher percentage on the front end product and then a smaller percentage on the back end product. That way, you both achieve what you wanted. You get a big response and the list owner makes money on the campaign.

Find out who the big list owners are in your field. Subscribe to their lists so you get an idea of the products they're promoting. And when you have your own product ready to go, try soliciting them with a JV proposal. If they see real value and an opportunity to make money, they might accept your proposal and send your offer out to tens of thousands of people.

Distribution Lists. In many industries, there are email distribution lists already established where you can send your email out for a flat fee. The nice thing about JV campaigns is that you only pay a percentage of revenue. If you sell nothing, it costs you nothing. With distribution lists, you pay a flat fee regardless of the response you get. *But* ... if you *do* make sales, you keep all the profit!

A good friend of mine sends out emails to a list of 60,000 prospective customers in the Promotional Products industry for a flat fee of just $275. I recently found a list of 72,000 Mortgage Brokers that you could email for $1800. That's a lot more than $275 but (depending on your sales) it's still a lot cheaper than a Joint Venture campaign.

You could also use a company like Majon.com. They have a list of over 20 million names and you can send an email to the whole bunch for about $2000. Obviously, you pay less when the list isn't filtered for a particular industry but it's still tempting to send an email to 20 million people!

Do some research. Put your keywords into a Google search along with the words "email distribution list" and see what comes up. You might be surprised at the result. In the case of my friend, he built his entire business with a single email campaign. That was four years ago and he's been doing it once each month ever since.

Think about the potential. What could *you* offer?

Resist the temptation to be greedy. Most people who are new to the internet are too quick to ask for money. The trend is towards providing more value upfront and building trust first.

Think about an irresistible offer; something anyone would want. You want the interaction. You want to engage your community. You want your audience to recognize who you are and become familiar with your name.

Interaction = Trust

The more they interact, the more they'll trust you. We'll talk more about this in later chapters but you need to treat this like a sales funnel. Offer tons of value at the beginning and build trust with your audience. You can profit from it later.

Email distribution lists are powerful opportunities to get your message out quickly and affordably. Do the research and see what you can find. Take a chance. It could change your business forever.

Step-by-step action guide:

- ☐ *Find the online gurus in your field.*
- ☐ *Subscribe to their email lists.*
- ☐ *Make note of the products they're selling.*
- ☐ *Google "email distribution lists".*
- ☐ *Identify irresistible offers for your audience.*
- ☐ *Build trust first, make money afterwards.*
- ☐ *Send out a huge email blast ... and wait.*

Email Distribution Lists

10

Keyword Ideas

Why reinvent the wheel? Your competitors can help!

This chapter (along with the next two) lays the foundation for your website. You might already have a website and that's great. But the vast majority of websites were built without this foundation in place. Once we've gone through the process, you'll probably have a very different perspective on what your website needs to do.

Let's dive in. On the internet, everything boils down to keywords. Everything is indexed according to keywords and a website that's built on efficient targeted keywords has a much better chance of being noticed, especially by search engines.

Did you know you can see exactly how your competitors built their own websites? It's true. You can visit any website you like, right click with your mouse (using Internet Explorer) and select View Source from the dropdown menu. Doing so opens a second window where all the code for that website is displayed.

Go try it. If you weren't aware of this, it'll amaze you.

But most people are already aware of this simple internet reality. So how can we benefit from it? Perhaps the biggest opportunity is that we can see exactly which keywords your competitors are targeting.

If you're on the homepage of a particular website and you click View Source, you'll notice a few lines of code at the top that start with "Meta Name". Usually, you'll find one for the site description and a second for the keywords being targeted.

Do a search for your ideal keywords and visit the sites that come up first in Google. After all, these websites are ranking at the top for the exact keywords *you're* targeting as well. Whatever keywords they're targeting are helping them achieve their impressive search engine rankings.

This is a great way to start building a list of potential keywords for your own website. Open a Word document and start copying and pasting all your competitor keywords from their websites into your document. It won't take long and you'll have a long list.

Go through the keywords and highlight the ones you like. Don't worry about narrowing the list too much. You can have as many as you like. But highlight the ones that relate most to your business.

In the next chapter, I'll introduce some powerful (and free) keyword research tools that can measure the targeting potential of your favorite keywords and give you suggestions for other related keywords as well.

For now, just make this big initial list and highlight the ones you like most. Then put those favorites at the top of the page in a larger font. We'll refine the list later, but it will form the foundation of your web presence.

Once you finalize your list, print it out and post it beside your computer. Every time you write something for your website or blog, look at your list. Use your keywords wherever possible. After a while, it will become second nature. But at the beginning, make sure you have your list nearby and etch those keywords into your mind.

In order for your website to be found by search engines like Google, it must offer content about the keywords you're targeting. Your list of keywords tells you exactly what information your website needs to offer.

Give the search engines what they're looking for. If you do, you'll be rewarded with better rankings. It's that simple. In Chapter 11, we'll identify those keywords that will be the easiest to conquer.

Step-by-step action guide:

- ☐ *Identify your ideal keywords and phrases.*
- ☐ *Search for those keywords on Google.*
- ☐ *Visit the homepages of the top websites.*
- ☐ *Right click and select View Source.*
- ☐ *Copy the keywords listed in the meta tags.*
- ☐ *Paste the keywords into a Word document.*
- ☐ *Highlight the keywords you like the most.*
- ☐ *Print the list with your favorites at the top.*
- ☐ *Post the list beside your computer screen.*

Keyword Ideas

11

Keyword Research

Where are the "sitting ducks"?

In Chapter 7, I mentioned the publicly accessible Google keyword selector tool. At that time, we used it to see what your customers are searching for. And I'll say it again: that's a very powerful tool to understand your market. It can identify opportunities you probably never would've thought of.

Anyway, you can find links to all the keyword research tools on the Tactical Execution website.

**Tactical Execution > Resources > Useful Links
> Keyword Research Links**

Regarding keywords, the ones you want to find are the *sitting ducks*! You want to find keyword phrases that have good organic search volume but limited competition. The Google keyword tool shows you both.

Once you've entered one of your primary keywords and pulled up the lists of related words, you can sort the results by competition and then scroll down to the bottom of the list. Down there, you'll find the keyword phrases that don't have that much competition and it's easy to see which ones still have good search volume.

By "competition", the Google keyword tool is talking about the pay-per-click competition for that word. You may not be interested in doing pay-per-click advertising and that's fine. But you can extrapolate the competition in the organic world from the competition in the PPC world. The two usually mirror each other.

Pick a few phrases that seem to have good search volume but limited competition and write them down. Then go to the WordTracker tool (also on the Tactical Execution website) and get an estimate of the daily search volume each phrase gets. That'll give you a good idea how many people are actually searching for each phrase.

WordTracker and Google run on different engines and you will find inconsistencies between them. That's okay. The idea is to get as much information as we can and then target the phrases that are the easiest to conquer.

I also recommend putting each phrase into a standard Google search with quotation marks around it. Make note of the total number of listings that come up for each. That gives you an even clearer idea of how many websites are discussing exactly that phrase.

The exact number of listings that come up isn't important. The important thing is to compare the number of listings for all the different keyword phrases you look up. Some have tons of listings while others have far less. The ones with the fewest listings are the easiest to rank high for because they have less competition.

These three simple steps allow you to identify the keyword phrases that are like "sitting ducks", just waiting for some attention. In fact, it's an extremely sophisticated research process and some companies regularly charge thousands of dollars to go through the process we just described.

I once picked a keyword phrase and got my website on page one of Google in just 17 days. The phrase was "growth marketing" and it didn't take much for my site to come up first. Why? Because the phrase "growth marketing" had almost no competition. This stuff works.

I promise you that at least 90% of companies never do proper keyword research for their websites even though it can make a massive difference. Efficient keywords are the most important building block for a successful online identity. Please don't miss this step. It's worth it.

One last note. I am generally a big proponent of doing things yourself. That's what this book is all about. And you can definitely do keyword research by yourself. But if you're in doubt at all, it's important enough that I would gladly pay a professional to get it right.

Tactical Execution offers keyword research packages.

Step-by-step action guide:

- ☐ *Visit the free Google Keyword Tool.*
- ☐ *Search your ideal keywords and phrases.*
- ☐ *Sort the results by 'Average Volume'.*
- ☐ *Look for good volume but low competition.*
- ☐ *Write down the attractive prospects.*
- ☐ *Visit the free WordTracker Keyword Tool.*
- ☐ *Get an estimate of daily search volume.*
- ☐ *Google each phrase with quotation marks.*
- ☐ *Note the total number of listings for each.*
- ☐ *Target best volume & lowest competition.*
- ☐ *Hire a professional if you're in doubt.*

Keyword Research

12

Positioning Statement

What's your Positioning Statement?

In Chapter 10, I encouraged you to visit your competitors' websites and get keyword ideas from their meta tags. I said you would probably find two lines of code (and maybe more) that started with "meta name"; one listing the keywords they're targeting and the other displaying a site description.

The last two chapters were all about the keywords. This chapter is all about the description. The description listed in the meta tags is the website's Positioning Statement.

Every website needs a 15 to 25-word Positioning Statement. It forms the foundation of the entire website. You need a focus and your Positioning Statement does that. In just 15 to 25 words, it needs to tell people exactly what you do.

Sounds a bit like an Elevator Pitch, doesn't it? Absolutely. In fact, it's just a shorter version. Your Elevator Pitch needs to be between 75 and 90 words long. Your Positioning Statement is between 15 and 25 words. And there's actually one more format – even shorter – and that's your Title Tag. It needs to be just 65 characters or less. We'll get to that in a second.

First, where do these statements show up?

If you do a Google search for anything, the organic listings are displayed in the center of the page. For every listing, there's a primary title you would click on to visit the website. Below that, you'll find a two-line description telling you what the page is about and the actual URL for the page is below that. Every listing has those four lines.

Your 65-character Title Tag is the primary title of the listing. Your 15 to 25-word Positioning Statement is the two-line description below the title and the URL is simply the location where that page resides.

Okay. Back to work. Get your Elevator Pitch from Chapter 6 and try to write a shorter version while incorporating the "sitting duck" keyword phrases you identified in Chapter 11. That's the goal. Explain exactly what you do in 15 to 25 words while using targeted keyword phrases.

Once you're finished, take the next step and summarize it further to a 65-character Title Tag.

Every page on your website should have a Title Tag and a description full of keywords and keyword phrases. It's important. If you do this correctly, your chances of ranking high up on Google skyrocket. We'll talk about this more in Chapter 45.

It's worth mentioning that your business focus might change from time to time – nothing wrong with that. Feel free to adjust it when necessary but always know that this keyword focus and strategic clarity plays a major role in your business' visibility on the internet.

Chapter 13 looks at a variety of different website development platforms. That's where all the keyword research, Title Tags and Positioning Statements come into play. That's where the rubber meets the road.

Hopefully, you're starting to see all the steps your competition is skipping. Most companies jump right in and start building their website. They only think about how they want it to look. Meanwhile, they skip the foundation and wonder why they don't show up on the search engines.

Take the steps I've laid out in these past three chapters. You only have to do them once and they'll pay dividends for as long as you have your website. It's worth it. I promise.

Step-by-step action guide:

- [ ] *Get your Elevator Pitch (Chapter 6).*
- [ ] *Get your targeted keywords (Chapter 11).*
- [ ] *Shorten your pitch to 15-25 words.*
- [ ] *Ensure it is full of your targeted keywords.*
- [ ] *This is your website Positioning Statement.*
- [ ] *Shorten it further to just 65 characters.*
- [ ] *Ensure it contains your primary keywords.*
- [ ] *This is your homepage Title Tag.*
- [ ] *Ensure every webpage has a Title Tag.*
- [ ] *Ensure every webpage has a description.*

Positioning Statement

13

Website Development

Build a killer website ... *for free!*

Yes, it's true. These days, there are countless options for you to build your very own website all by yourself. And it doesn't mean you have to settle for some amateur-looking site either.

Let's start with the heavy-weights. There are a variety of platforms that are referred to as "open source", meaning they were developed under the GNU (or general public license) and they are entirely free to use.

Although open source had its beginnings back in the 60s, the term became more widely used after Netscape released its source code in 1998. Today, open source refers to software developed by and for the public. Anyone can contribute to it and anyone can use it. No charge.

These open source website platforms are often referred to as "web application frameworks" or "content management systems" and they allow you to build impressive websites through a backend administrative interface (also called a dashboard or control panel).

Although these platforms all vary slightly, their interfaces have buttons like "create a page" or "insert an image" or "add a link", allowing you to build your website from the ground up, one page at a time.

There are three primary platforms in this area: Joomla, Drupal and WordPress. Joomla is the most powerful but also the most complicated. WordPress is less powerful but incorporates blog functionality and is probably (statistics are hard to find) the most heavily used. Drupal is essentially in the middle in terms of functionality and 3rd place in terms of usage.

The Tactical Execution website is built on WordPress and I haven't spent a dime on it so far. I did it all myself. Even the graphic images were free. I either created them in Word or found them on public clipart databases. Amateur, I admit, but it works.

Within one month of installing WordPress for the very first time, my website already had over 250 pages of content, improving it's ranking with the search engines. I was able to quickly add pages and copy in content I had created for other purposes beforehand.

Is my website among the best on the internet? Absolutely not. But it's doing exactly what I need it to do and I was able to build it myself. Freedom! In fact, with some of the widgets and resource tools available these days, you can make your site look pretty impressive and it's only going to get easier as time passes.

Check out www.widgetbox.com to get a taste.

I'm obviously a big fan of open source platforms but there are other options as well. For starters, both Microsoft and Google have introduced website-building platforms and are eager to find new users. Microsoft Office Live and Google Sites are both free platforms and are well integrated with their related applications.

Most large hosting companies also have website-building platforms they offer to their customers. Most of them charge a higher monthly hosting fee if your site is built on their platform and I discourage you from using them. There are just too many free alternatives to choose from.

The trend is clear. Everyone is trying to provide easier ways for average people to build impressive websites. Personally, I think it makes the most sense to align yourself with an open source platform like WordPress and let the technology push you forward.

Step-by-step action guide:

- ☐ *Look into WordPress, Joomla and Drupal.*
- ☐ *Research each to see which you like best.*
- ☐ *Visit the Microsoft Office Live website.*
- ☐ *Visit the Google Sites website.*
- ☐ *Visit your hosting company's website.*
- ☐ *Commit to one platform and get started.*
- ☐ *Start slow and build one page at a time.*
- ☐ *Grow and improve your site as you learn.*

Website Development

14

Website Sales Function

Is your website making sales?

Probably not. I mean; maybe it is, but most aren't. The vast majority of websites do *not* do a good job converting visitors into happy paying customers.

Your website is part of your Sales Department. Driving traffic to your website, on the other hand, is part of your Marketing Department. That's an important distinction. We'll talk about driving traffic at the end of this book. For now, let's talk about the sales function.

Once your website is discovered by a first-time visitor, it needs to have a 'conversation' with that person. It needs to identify the problem and how you can solve it. It needs to introduce your products and it needs to close the sale. If it doesn't, it's not doing its job.

If you browse around the internet, you'll find lots of beautiful well-designed websites, but that doesn't mean they convert well. In fact, some of the most basic websites convert the best. Why? Because they're so easy to understand.

Let's look at three questions your website must answer within the first five seconds. Why five seconds? Because that's about how much time you have before a first-time visitor decides whether he or she wants to continue browsing your site or click the Back button.

1. Why am I here?

Visitors to your site need to understand why they're there. They need to see an explanation of what you *do* right at the top of the homepage. And guess what? That's why we worked on your Elevator Pitch in Chapter 6. That's why we crafted your Positioning Statement and your Title Tag.

Your Title Tag should be the lead statement on your homepage; the words in the biggest font. After that, your slightly-longer Positioning Statement comes next, elaborating on your Title Tag. And depending on your website layout, you might even include your entire Elevator Pitch, fleshing out your value proposition even further.

People need to know what you do. Tell them. They're browsing the internet for a reason. They're looking for something and it's either on your site or it's not. They need to know if you have what they're looking for and they need to know quickly.

2. Where do I look?

Most websites have far too many options on the homepage. It's confusing. People's eyes glaze over and they lose focus. Studies have been done on this. It's called eye tracking. Too many options destroy your website's "eye flow" and there's no such thing as a confused buyer.

The purpose of your homepage is to navigate visitors into the bowels of your website. It's to get them to a place where their questions are answered. It's to get them to a place where they can find what they're looking for.

Give your homepage only a small number of buttons to choose from. Here are a few two-button examples.

[I am a man]   or   [I am a woman]
[I am a buyer]   or   [I am a seller]
[I am an individual] or   [I am a business]

These are simple navigational buttons that get visitors to the right place. Figure out what the basic distinctions are for *your* business; the main categories you sell to. Then use your homepage to tell your visitors what you do and navigate them to the right place.

3. What do I do?

Always tell your visitors what to do next. When people visit your website, they are in a submissive position. They are in a receiving mode. They have no control over what they're about to see. You do. That's a huge opportunity that most companies never take advantage of.

Tell them what to do. Click here to learn more. Call us for a free estimate. Register for our next workshop. Get a quote today. Apply now. These are all vitally important instructions. They're all calls-to-action. Your visitors might be interested or they might not. You'll never know if you don't ask.

Demonstrate confidence on your website. Ask for the sale in no uncertain terms. If your websites projects confidence, your visitors automatically assume you're more credible. A timid website does the opposite.

My Tactical Execution website is no award-winner but you can see my efforts to use this same advice. My homepage gives people a few clear choices and each one leads to a different part of my site. I'm trying to navigate my visitors quickly, getting them to a place where they can find what they're looking for – hopefully!

Spend some time thinking about this *before* you build your website. It's a lot easier to build a new site than fix an old broken one. Done properly, your website does the sales job it's designed for and that's when the fun starts.

Step-by-step action guide:

- ☐ *Your website is in your Sales Department.*
- ☐ *Generating website traffic is Marketing.*
- ☐ *Think about first-time visitors to your site.*
- ☐ *Identify exactly what you want them to do.*
- ☐ *Answer three questions in five seconds.*
- ☐ *Why am I here? Tell them what you do.*
- ☐ *Where do I look? Offer a few clear choices.*
- ☐ *What do I do? Tell them what to do next.*
- ☐ *Think about this **before** you start building.*

Website Sales Function

15

Website Cornerstone: Focus

What makes a great website?

There are basically three cornerstones to an effective website; three things that encompass everything a website needs, not only to cater to human beings but to search engines as well.

1. Focus
2. Depth
3. Value

We'll be talking about the first one in this chapter. We'll talk about Depth in the next chapter and Value in the chapter after that. By structuring your website according to these three cornerstones, you'll be well positioned to capitalize on today's internet economy.

Focus essentially refers to the keywords your website is built on. And it's a critically important part of any successful online strategy. Yet, it's counter-intuitive for most people and goes against their natural instincts. Follow along with me for a moment.

Most people feel like they're restricting themselves if they focus their website too much. They feel like they're walking away from potential business by pigeonholing themselves with a narrow focus. And while that has a certain intuitive appeal, it doesn't work well online.

Let's assume you're a Financial Advisor who's trying to sell annuities, life insurance and estate planning services. If you built your website balanced between those three and if someone was searching for life insurance, the search engines would see that roughly 33% of your website offers information about that topic. Do you think you would come up first? If there was another website that was 100% devoted to life insurance, do you think it would come up higher than yours? Likely.

The search engines look for density of unique relevant content as defined by the words used in the search query and related words. If only 33% of your website relates to the words used in the search query, your website comes up lower than all the other websites that are more exclusively devoted to that topic. That's an over-simplification but you get the point.

Now, if you came up on page #17 in the search engine results for three different topics, do you think you'll be getting any traffic from search engines? No. Absolutely not. Nobody even gets past page #2 or #3, at least not for 99% of searches. On the other hand, if you came up on page #1 or #2 in the search engine, do you think you'll be getting traffic as a result? The answer is YES.

There's a saying in Internet Marketing that says "go an inch wide and a mile deep." That means you're better off selecting a narrow topic and then building a massive website around it. We'll be going over the "massive" part in the next chapter (Depth) but the narrow focus is critical.

Now, let's get back to our example. If you specialized only in life insurance and came up on page #2 as a result, and if someone found you by searching for life insurance on a search engine, do you think you might get a chance to cross sell them other services like annuities and estate planning later on? Of course.

Your specialty is simply intended to get them in the door. You can even devote a small part of your website to the other services you offer; just make sure you keep the overwhelming focus on your primary specialty.

One of my problems with Tactical Execution is that my site is too broad. It has a ton of information about internet marketing but there's also information about traditional marketing, real estate mortgages, the stock market and the economy. Of course, I also focus on my speaking career and have pages devoted to that. It's not specialized enough for modern search engines.

I built a website for a bank and the entire website was devoted to their real estate division specializing in 1031 exchanges (for investment properties). The website is extremely focused.

At the time of this writing, that website has 94 pages and my Tactical Execution website has over 500 pages but their website gets more than twice as much organic search engine traffic as my website gets. You would think the volume of my content would win. Nope. Their focus wins.

Obviously, a website with both content *and* focus offers the best alternative but this comparison illustrates the point. Focus is critically important for a successful website.

Think about your business. Think about your expertise and select an area where you can become a true authority. Use the keyword research tools we discussed in Chapter 11 to identify the most efficient keyword phrases and then build your website around that narrow focus.

The next chapter is all about Depth and it deals precisely with the volume of content on your website. It's the second cornerstone of an effective website.

Step-by-step action guide:

- ☐ Select one focused area to specialize in.
- ☐ Review your targeted keyword phrases.
- ☐ Build your website as focused as possible.
- ☐ Resist the instinct to cover everything.
- ☐ Ensure one keyword phrase dominates.
- ☐ Cross sell other products or services later.

Website Cornerstone: Focus

16

Website Cornerstone: Depth

What's the easiest way to accumulate massive content for your website?

That's not an easy question to answer but we'll look at a few ideas in a second. First, let's get back to the three cornerstones of an effective website and review our progress. The three cornerstones are:

1. Focus
2. Depth
3. Value

In Chapter 15, we discussed Focus and importance of selecting one specialty to form the foundation of your online identity. In this chapter, we'll move on to the second cornerstone: Depth.

When someone puts a few keywords into a search query, the search engines look out into the internet and deliver websites that have a large quantity of unique relevant content containing the keywords entered along with words that are related to the keywords entered.

Incidentally, if you're curious how the search engines know what words are related to the keywords entered, they just look into their user history database and see what other words were commonly included in searches that contained the same keywords that were used by the current user.

If someone searches for the word "mortgage", the search engines quickly see that other searchers included words like "refinance" and "purchase" when the word "mortgage" was also used. As a result, they know "mortgage", "refinance" and "purchase" are all related words.

Bottom line; the more content you have on your website about those keywords, the more likely you are to come up high on the search engines results page. So how do you accumulate massive content? That depends on whether or not you like to write and produce content.

It's pretty obvious that I like to produce content. I add new content to my website almost every day and I enjoy it. So if you're like me, let me offer a word to the wise. I recommend writing an outline of all the topics you could cover *before* you start writing. The reason is simple. Without an outline, all the knowledge in your head is inter-related. If you just start writing, you'll peripherally mention too many different things too quickly. After just three or four posts, you'll run out of things to say.

Write an outline first. By doing so, you'll force your mind to organize the knowledge you have and structure it into a series of specific topics. In fact, you'll probably find yourself subdividing topics into more and more minute details you could cover. Within an hour or two, you could easily have a list of 50 to 60 topics you could cover. After that, any time you have some extra time, just pull out your list, select a topic to write about and cross it off your list.

If you hate writing or find that you just don't have that much to say, I offer two suggestions. First, go to a website like EzineArticles.com and do some searches for your favorite keywords. You'll quickly find hundreds or even thousands of articles about those keywords. You can use these articles as inspiration for your own efforts. They can give you a ton of ideas quickly.

You can also post these articles directly on your own website as long as you include the author resource box, linking back to the author's website. That's the way it works. That's what those authors are looking for. They'll be thrilled with the added exposure.

If you decide to publish other people's articles on your own website, don't expect them to improve your rankings with Google. Search engines look for duplicate content when indexing the internet so your reproduced articles won't count for anything except information for your visitors.

My second suggestion is to get others to create content on your behalf. I have two clients who are accepting articles written by their customers for inclusion on their respective blogs. Both parties win. The customers get a chance to demonstrate their expertise in front of a new audience and my clients get unique relevant content for their websites.

You can also hire young writers to blog on your behalf. This cutting-edge marketing strategy has taken no-name companies to prominence in record time. You could hire a few 23-year-old college graduates to write for your company blog and have a ton of content overnight.

At the beginning, pay them per post. In time, bonus them according to the amount of traffic their posts receive and the amount of time their visitors spend on the site. It's easy to track and we'll be discussing tools like Google Analytics in more detail in Chapter 34.

One way or another, if you want your website to get high rankings by the search engines, you need to build massive unique relevant content around your narrow focus. Think about which strategy works for you and start accumulating content today!

One last note: never take content away. Only add. Always add. Over time, you want your website to grow and grow. That's the beauty of blogs – just keep adding more. We'll talk more about blogs starting in Chapter 22.

Step-by-step action guide:

- ☐ *Create an outline of topics you can cover.*
- ☐ *Subdivide your topics as much as possible.*
- ☐ *Write about a topic when you have time.*
- ☐ *Visit EzineArticles.com to get ideas.*
- ☐ *Consider publishing other people's articles.*
- ☐ *Invite your clients to contribute content.*
- ☐ *Consider hiring people to write content.*
- ☐ *Pay bonuses for high-traffic posts.*
- ☐ *Never remove content. Always add more.*

Website Cornerstone: Depth

17

Website Cornerstone: Value

Why would your website visitors come back to your site again and again? The answer is Value.

If they get value from your website, they'll come back a second time and a third. More importantly, they'll tell their friends about it and that endorsement is worth far more than any advertising you might be doing! But before we get into the details, let's get back to the three cornerstones of an effective website and review our progress.

1. Focus
2. Depth
3. Value

In Chapter 15, we discussed Focus and the importance of selecting one specialty as the foundation for your online identity. In Chapter 16, we discussed Depth and how to accumulate massive content on your website. In this chapter, we'll finish it off with a discussion about Value. Generally speaking, value comes in one of three forms.

1. Updating Content
2. Value Items
3. Resource Tools

Updating Content refers to those pieces of data that change over time and that can be updated automatically on your website. Interest rates. Stock market values. Real estate values. Horoscopes. News feeds. Blog posts. Podcasts. Birthday reminders. These are all examples of content that change on a regular basis. If a website had one of these examples, you could visit the same site on different days and get different content each time.

Obviously, the type of content you could display on your website would depend on your field but I encourage you to think about things you could post on your website that would (hopefully) update automatically. These days, a lot of web platforms offer fancy widgets you can add to your website quickly and easily. Check out widgetbox.com and search for widgets in your field. That way, you could incorporate updating content on your website without having to update it yourself.

Blogs are an excellent example of updating content and the best part is that you are in complete control over the content you're offering. Is it more work than a widget? Yes. But the possible upside is bigger as well. Blogs are a powerful tool in modern marketing and you might want to consider including that in your marketing strategy. We'll talk more about that starting in Chapter 22.

Value Items include things of significance people can get on your website. It might be a free white paper about your field. It might be a few instructional videos to help them achieve one thing or another. It might be a series of educational articles or a PDF document with important definitions in your industry.

From a slightly more sophisticated perspective, it could be a Facebook application. It could be a fancy MySpace template. It could be a WordPress theme or a unique ring tone. Of course, these examples involve some actual coding but the marketing potential is huge and many companies are building their audiences by offering these sophisticated Value Items to their website visitors.

Resource Tools include any web-based functionality that helps you do something. You can imagine how many examples there are of this. At the simplest level, resource tools might include mortgage payment calculators and calorie counters. On the more sophisticated end, it would include any of the web platforms designed to help you run your life. Sites like OpenTable.com, BaseCamp.com and all the online banking platforms come to mind.

Again, these last examples all involve extensive coding to create. But that doesn't mean you can't offer your audience tools they can use. In many cases, you can use widgets hosted by other platforms and incorporate those into your website. Again, visit widgetbox.com and do a search for your favorite keywords. You might be surprised how many resource tools are available and most of them are absolutely free.

Updating Content, Value Items and Resource Tools all represent things you can offer to bring your website visitors back again and again. Get creative with the ideas we've discussed here and develop your own proprietary blend of value to push out to your audience. It all helps to build your traffic and solidify your position as an authority in your field.

Focus, Depth and Value are the cornerstones of an effective website. The last three chapters dealt with each in turn. Keep these concepts in your mind as you build out your online identity, not just your website but your internet activities in general. Let them act as enduring guideposts for your journey and they will ensure you always have the end in mind.

Step-by-step action guide:

- ☐ *Consider Updating Content in your field.*
- ☐ *Think about information you could offer.*
- ☐ *Visit widgetbox.com to look for examples.*
- ☐ *Consider Value Items you could offer.*
- ☐ *Allocate time to create these Value Items.*
- ☐ *Consider Resource Tools you could offer.*
- ☐ *Incorporate functionality on your website.*
- ☐ *Let Focus, Depth & Value define your site.*

Website Cornerstone: Value

18

Website Conversation

What do you want your website visitors to learn about you?

Whenever someone stumbles upon your website, a 'conversation' is taking place. In fact, before the conversation even starts, there's a first impression; just like the offline world. You need to take these dynamics into consideration and build your website accordingly.

Let's start with the first impression. This relates to the lesson we covered in Chapter 14. Why am I here? Your website needs to answer that question right away. Your visitors need to find out if your website has what they are looking for ... or not.

The way to do that is to put your Positioning Statement front and center on your homepage and then offer a few clear choices for them to navigate to an area of the website that addresses their needs. If they click on one of those choices, they just told you that they still believe your website has what they are looking for. That's great news!

This is where the conversation starts taking shape. As visitors navigate through your website, they learn things about you. They learn what you do and what you offer.

You have control over what they learn, and in what order. Yet, few business owners take advantage of that opportunity.

Whether you already have a website or not, take some time to write down a series of statements that you'd like your website visitors to learn about you. Don't worry which are the most important or what order they should be in. Just write them down. Try to come up with at least 10 statements that you would like them to think about when they think about you.

1. Tactical Execution offers tested marketing strategies for small business.
2. Tactical Execution has a ton of useful free resources available on its website.
3. Tactical Execution provides solutions that can help entrepreneurs build their businesses.

You get the idea. Allocate some time and do the exercise. Make a list and then put them in a logical order. What do you want them to learn first? Second? Third? These statements form the pages that navigate your website visitors through your site. At some point, the next thing your visitors learn might depend on who they are. In other words, there may be a fork in the road.

Chapter 14 discussed how your homepage should navigate your visitors into the bowels of your site, to a location that addresses their needs. Often, your secondary pages do the same thing, segmenting your visitors even further. Depending on the selections they make, your visitors might end up in a dozen different locations on your site.

Each page needs to communicate a clear message to the visitor. As the pages divide visitors according to their selections, so too must your website address their increasingly qualified needs. A conversation is taking place and you can script your side of it the same way some companies use scripts for customer service phone calls.

Most websites are like unkempt fields completely overgrown with weeds and bushes; stuff everywhere with no real rhyme or reason. Think about chopping a path through that field. That's essentially what you're doing. You're building a path for your visitors to walk on. Along the way, you can decide what they see and what they learn. You can even put some carrots along the way, slowly guiding them to the purchase page.

Chapter 17 discussed the third cornerstone of an effective website: Value. These are the carrots along your path. These are the things that encourage interaction and build trust. Interaction = trust. The more you can get your visitors to interact with your website, the more they trust you as a provider.

I know this might sound esoteric but the concept is important. You have complete control over your website. You control what's on the homepage and you control what's on all the other pages as well. Take advantage of that opportunity! Figure out what you want them to learn and then build a path for them to walk on. If you do, it will dramatically improve the conversion rate your website delivers.

Step-by-step action guide:

- ☐ *Your website is in your Sales Department.*
- ☐ *Decide what your visitors should learn.*
- ☐ *Plan the conversation your website has.*
- ☐ *Qualify your website visitors on each page.*
- ☐ *Always craft your message to the visitor.*
- ☐ *Build a "path" for your visitors to walk on.*
- ☐ *Encourage interaction along the way.*

Website Conversation

19

Email Marketing

Email List = Audience = Influence = Revenue

We touched on email distribution lists back in Chapter 9. Here, we'll go into a lot more detail.

Email marketing is one of the most powerful tools for modern businesses. Not only can you deliver messages with absolutely zero delivery costs but you can touch your audience multiple times, establishing trust as you go.

This book started as an email course and it's still available in that format on the Tactical Execution website. You get all the same information (except for six bonus chapters, a suggested weekly execution plan and the itemized to-do lists) as 52 weekly emails. So if you don't mind waiting a full year, you can get the same information for free.

The beauty of that course is that the individual emails are all sent automatically from an online platform. It's called an Email Autoresponder and it's one of the most powerful tools for internet marketers. You write the emails at the beginning and then upload them to the platform. After that, they get sent out automatically according to a predetermined time lapse schedule.

That means that while one person is receiving email #19, another person might be receiving email #2 or email #49. It's all happening at the same time and you don't have to do a thing. As long as the emails are written and uploaded to the platform, your job is done. At the same time, the people on your list get the information in the perfect order and on a predictable schedule.

Have you ever heard of the Rule of Seven? It says that people need to be touched by your message seven different times before they remember it and recognize you. In the good old days, that meant you had to send your audience seven direct mail pieces or hit them with seven marketing messages before you could expect respectable results. Today, it means you have to send seven emails before they start trusting you.

Email Autoresponders are the perfect tool to accomplish this. This is the 19th chapter of this book. In the email course, it's Tip #18. By that point, recipients know a lot more about Tactical Execution than they did at the start. They know the type of information they're getting. They know the approach we espouse. And they know the style of our delivery.

You can obviously use an Autoresponder for your own marketing as well. Think about your business and what value you could push to your audience. Pretend you're a teacher and your prospects are your students. What can you teach them? How can you benefit their lives? Start writing an outline of all the lessons you'd like to cover.

You don't need to have them all written by the time you launch the program. Do you think I had all 52 emails written when I first accepted subscriptions on my website? Absolutely not. I only had two emails written at that point. The rest I wrote later. I only needed to stay ahead of the first subscriber to keep it seamless.

Here's a good analogy. Maybe you've heard this one before. Here goes. If you and a friend are in the woods and you're both being chased by a bear, you really don't need to run faster than the bear. You only need to run faster than your friend. As long as you run faster than your buddy, you're in good shape!

Same goes for an Email Autoresponder. Don't worry about building the whole program before you launch. That's too much work. Instead, create your outline and write the first two or three emails. Then, allocate some time to write more and more, posting them all to the online platform. Before you know it, you'll have the whole thing done and can relax while your list continues to grow.

Email lists are powerful tools. They give you a way of sending a message with zero delivery expense. You own an audience. The cast of the popular television show "Friends" earned $1MM each per episode during the last two seasons. Why? Because they owned an audience. They created an opportunity for advertisers.

The same is true for email lists. If you have a list of 10,000 or 20,000 email addresses, you own an audience. You have what everyone else wants. I know one internet marketer who has over 800,000 email subscribers. A big email list gives you the power to promote other people's products and get a generous commission on the sale.

Remember Chapter 9? We talked about Joint Ventures and large email distribution lists. With an Email Autoresponder, you can build a list of your own and then provide endorsements for others who are trying to promote their products.

In the case of information products (like e-books, CDs or DVDs), your endorsement combined with your email list can earn you as much as 50% or 75% of the product's sales price. It's an incredibly powerful tool and one that can help you make a fortune online.

Although there are dozens of different platforms available, the two leading providers are Constant Contact and Aweber. Both links are listed on the Tactical Execution website.

**Tactical Execution > Resources > Useful Links
     > Marketing Links**

I use Aweber for the email course on my website. Check it out, and see if you can incorporate this powerful internet marketing tool into your own business.

Step-by-step action guide:

- ☐ *Pretend you're a teacher with expertise.*
- ☐ *Pretend your prospects are your students.*
- ☐ *Think about the lessons you could deliver.*
- ☐ *Create an outline for a series of lessons.*
- ☐ *Write out the first two or three lessons.*
- ☐ *Google "email autoresponders" to research.*
- ☐ *Visit Aweber and Constant Contact as well.*
- ☐ *Decide which platform you'd like to use.*
- ☐ *Upload the initial lessons to your account.*
- ☐ *Create a sign-up web form (easy to do).*
- ☐ *Put the sign-up form on your homepage.*
- ☐ *Promote your program to get subscribers.*

Email Marketing

20

Expand the Frame

How do you take your business to the next level?

In this chapter, we borrow some concepts from social dynamics theory to dramatically expand the frame of your business. Let me start with a quick story.

A past client of mine has a business selling wine jelly. Yes, that's right. Wine jelly. Apparently, it tastes really good. But that's not the point. Before we met, his website had products ranging in price from $4 to $28. They included different sized jars and one package deal with four large jars. Now, picture what you might think when you stumble upon his website.

If it were me, I would picture a retail shelf vendor and nothing more. I would picture a few jars with a particular label sitting there on the shelf, beside dozens of competitive products. There is absolutely nothing that would jump out at me. And that's precisely the problem. He was a retail shelf vendor and nothing more.

After working together, we introduced a once-annual three-day retreat up in Napa, including an extensive tour of a winery on one day, an afternoon workshop on a second day (teaching participants how to make wine jelly in their own homes) and three gourmet meals per day, each featuring wine jelly in one fashion or another. The price for the retreat is $3995 and it's featured on his homepage. Now, picture yourself once again as you discover this website.

In the first case, you have found a retail shelf vendor selling little jars of jelly. In the second scenario, you have found a parallel universe that you never knew existed; a world full of romance, passion and good food. You have discovered a world you have never seen, a potential hobby and a rich addition to your life. It's a totally different frame. It's a totally different experience.

Keep in mind; nobody needs to buy the retreat package, at least not at the beginning.

When someone clicks onto your website, they are in the submissive position. They are in a receiving mode. They have absolutely no control over what they are about to see. You do. We talked about this in Chapter 18. You control everything they see. You control the frame.

That's a huge opportunity that few businesses take advantage of. You can present a small timid frame with your little product or service available for sale. Or you can present a huge overwhelming presence full of opportunities to change people's lives. It's your choice.

Think bigger. Expand the frame of your business. Think about the personal objectives of your prospective customers. They are people. They have their own goals and passions. Think of ways to let them pursue their own objectives within the context of your business. Cater to their inner most desires. Cater to their human side. Cater to their emotions.

Don't ever underestimate the passion of your customers. They might not all buy what you're offering. That's okay. But some will. Trust me. Some will. You'll see. Some will engage and see your business as a way for them to improve their own lives.

Cater to them! Build your business for them. They have friends. And if your business is improving their lives, you can bet they'll be telling their friends. And some of your other less-passionate customers might just get a bit jealous and engage more themselves.

Another great example is what Barack Obama has been doing online. I don't care if you like his politics or if you hate his politics. That's not what I'm talking about. But during his campaign, he created a website that allowed supporters to get involved in an incredibly productive way.

They could have 'friends', create a 'neighborhood', attend events and even organize their own events. They could even start their very own blog right on *his* platform and if they did, they'd have one of over 60,000 individual blogs created by his supporters.

Whether you like his politics or not, Barack Obama gave his supporters an opportunity to achieve their objectives within his campaign. Some people wanted to become 'big wigs' in his campaign and his platform gave them a way to do it. Others wanted to organize local events. His platform gave them the tools. Some wanted to encourage others to donate money. His website gave them a way to match funds for new donors. Others just wanted to meet people with similar political interests and Barack Obama's website provided a social network for his supporters to connect with each other.

There's a moral to these stories. Think bigger. Redefine what you do. Include your customers' personal objectives into your business model. They'll be happier and so will you. Present an overwhelming online identity and watch your customer interactions change forever!

I am using this same strategy when I invite you to start your own local **Web**ify **Business Club**, mentioned in the first chapter and again in Chapter 58. Independent professionals are desperate for the information in this book and they're looking for productive networking opportunities as well. You can fill both needs while positioning yourself at the center of your local entrepreneur community.

http://www.WebifyClub.com/

I'll email you a PDF agenda and worksheet to accompany each chapter and you can use Meetup.com to quickly find local professionals who are searching for this information. By doing so, I'm expanding the frame of this book and giving the community a tangible way to bring these pages to life. Read Chapter 58 for more details.

Step-by-step action guide:

- [ ] *Consider your customers' personal lives.*
- [ ] *List their passions & personal objectives.*
- [ ] *Brainstorm ways to cater to that list.*
- [ ] *Think bigger about your business model.*
- [ ] *Offer products with higher price points.*
- [ ] *Don't worry if people buy them or not.*
- [ ] *Promote your most extravagant product.*
- [ ] *See who responds and solicit feedback.*
- [ ] *Calibrate your product offering.*
- [ ] *Present an overwhelming online identity.*
- [ ] *Offer your product menu with confidence.*
- [ ] *Expand the frame of your business!*

Expand the Frame

21

Speak to Your Audience

Does your website *speak* to your audience?

I mean literally. Does it *speak*??

Turns out, there are some very simple things you can do to increase the level of trust first-time visitors have with your website. Let's take a look.

It was proven long ago that a statement is immediately deemed more credible if it is accompanied with a photo. That's why testimonials commonly have photos of the person right beside the words. When people can see a photo, the words become real. Readers can identify with the message quicker.

Audio and video have an even larger effect. As the medium becomes richer, so does the trust level among people reading, listening or watching. The easier it is for them to *identify* with the source, the easier it is for them to *trust* the source. And as we all know, people have to trust you before they'll be willing to buy anything.

What if a visitor to your website was immediately greeted by a short audio welcome message from you, the owner?

What if that message also told them the most valuable thing available on your website? Do you think that might change your conversion rate? Do you think it might keep your visitors browsing a bit longer?

What if the visitor was greeted by a video?

Adding audio and video content to your website has never been easier. With audio, you need little more than a decent microphone. The software is free. For Mac users, it's called Garage Band and for PC users, there are a number of options but I recommend Audacity. You can download and install Audacity in seconds, just by entering "audacity recording software" in a Google search.

I recommend spending a few dollars on the microphone. They range in price from about $10 to $600. I'm not suggesting you need to spend $600 but I do recommend getting something in the $50 range. The difference in sound quality is noticeable.

There are two other things you'll need. First, pick up a stand for your new microphone. It's worth the money. It keeps the microphone steady while you deliver your message and that helps to keep your recording volume even throughout your message.

Secondly, you absolutely *must* get a "pop filter". And what's that? It looks like a large foam rubber ball that fits on the top of your microphone. Without it, your P's, B's and D's pop into the microphone and later pop into the listeners' ears. It's distracting.

Hold your hand up to your mouth and say the word "podcast". You'll feel the air hit your hand when you say the P. Without the foam rubber to divert that air, the microphone picks it up as a loud pop. You can buy a pop filter for less than $10 and it will eliminate those pops.

I also recommend using effects like Compression and Base Boost to improve the sound quality. I use both effects on my own recordings and they round out my voice and make it sound smooth and buttery, like a radio announcer!!

If you configure the audio to begin playing automatically when someone visits your website, I suggest you make it short and sweet. You might surprise some people who could be sitting at their desk at work! On the other hand, if the visitor can start and stop the audio file manually, it can be as long as you like.

Video represents another incredible opportunity. Again, the software is free. Mac users have iMovie and PC users have Windows Movie Maker. Once made, websites like YouTube allow you to upload videos and then embed them directly onto your website. In other words, you don't need to worry about coding a video player onto your website. We'll talk about video more in Chapter 54.

More and more websites are incorporating audio and video content for their visitors. Companies are realizing that rich media formats dramatically increase the trust level visitors have when they visit a website. And the costs have come down dramatically. Take advantage of the opportunity and add a personal audio or video message to your website.

Step-by-step action guide:

- ☐ *Consider including audio on your website.*
- ☐ *Buy a $50 microphone to start recording.*
- ☐ *Get a stand and a $10 pop filter as well.*
- ☐ *PC users; download and install Audacity.*
- ☐ *Record a short welcome message.*
- ☐ *Use Compression and Base Boost effects.*
- ☐ *Add your audio message to your website.*

Speak to Your Audience

22

The Blogosphere

Do you hate the word "blog"?

For a lot of people, the word *blog* represents a younger generation they don't understand, technology they find intimidating and an internet culture that's passing them by.

Whether you *love* blogs or *hate* blogs, the facts speak for themselves. Blogs get more traffic. Blogs are favored by the search engines and all the latest and greatest online tools cater directly to blogs. Bottom line; if you're not blogging, you're missing out on most of today's internet opportunities.

If you're not that familiar with blogs, they look a lot like websites. In fact, you've probably been on a bunch of blogs and not even realized it. The difference is in the plumbing. The information is organized differently but the blog 'culture' represents another significant departure from the old static websites that used to dominate the internet.

The next six chapters discuss blogs and how you can use them to leverage your content, your community and the social media platforms that bind them together. In this chapter, it's important to introduce blogs by explaining why they're so heavily favored by the search engines.

Search engines look for three primary things when evaluating different websites. Blogs cater to all three.

1. The quantity of unique relevant content.
2. The newness or freshness of that content.
3. The link structure surrounding the website.

Blogs are basically online journals and their authors add more content on a regular (sometimes daily) basis. Over time, some blogs accumulate hundreds or even thousands of individual posts, catering directly to the first two things search engines look for.

Next, the culture in the blogosphere is to link out to as many other resources as you possibly can, including other bloggers. Bloggers are fiercely loyal to other bloggers! That means popular blog posts can end up with hundreds of inbound links coming from other blogs. That satisfies the last requirement search engines have.

The net result is that blogs are coming up higher and higher on search engine rankings. That means they're getting more organic traffic from the search engines and more exposure in general.

Let me repeat something I said first in Chapter 13. WordPress offers a way for anybody to start blogging without paying a penny. It's an open source platform and is available for anyone to use.

Tactical Execution offers a complete WordPress website & blog installation package that includes a theme, 10 essential plugins, a basic static page hierarchy and blog tab already published. It also comes with detailed instructions for using WordPress effectively.

Tactical Execution > Services > WordPress Package

The Tactical Execution website was built using WordPress. As of January 2009, the site had over 500 pages of content, and it didn't cost me a dime. And even though my knowledge of HTML is minimal, I was able to build the entire website myself.

Blogs cater to those who enjoy producing content. Many people don't like to write. Fear not. Starting in Chapter 29, we'll review some powerful options that don't require you to write long blog posts everyday.

The last thing I'll mention in this chapter is that you can easily hire other people to blog on your behalf. New and innovative companies have adopted these strategies to gain online exposure and it's working like a charm. We talked about this in Chapter 16.

Put an ad on Craig's List or Google for "ghost writers" and hire some young college students to blog about your field. You could pay them per post and bonus them based on the traffic their posts receive. It's performance-based compensation and adds directly to your website traffic, your revenue and your profits.

Step-by-step action guide:

 Blogs are favored by search engines.
Consider building a blog-based website.
WordPress is a popular open source option.
Potentially hire others to write content.

The Blogosphere

23

Blog Directories

Does anyone know you exist?

If you're like most bloggers, the answer is NO. A lot of talented 'content creators' publish inspiring blog posts that nobody ever reads! Sad but true.

The next five chapters discuss Blogging Best Practices and how you can share your brilliance with a global audience. And it all begins with awareness. If nobody knows you exist, they have no way of endorsing your content and sharing it with their friends.

Today's internet offers ever-expanding social media platforms where you can share your content with the world. But before we talk about those platforms in detail, we need to address the basics.

There are hundreds of free blog directories on the internet. You need to get registered on as many of those as you can. Will it drive hundreds of unique visitors to your site? No, it won't. But it announces to the internet world that you exist. Bottom line; you want to be listed in any place where somebody might find you.

In preparation for the project, you need to put some thought into your blog title and description. Even for those who have already finalized those details, it's worth taking a minute to rethink them. The description, in particular, is extremely valuable real estate and you want it to pull readers in with curiosity.

Every blog directory requests your blog title and your blog description. Make sure you have them in place before you get started.

A lot of people might tell you that the inbound links from these directories boost your search engine ranking. My response to that: maybe. The search engines have largely discounted links from directories so I wouldn't expect too much. The main benefit is simply to populate the internet with your existence.

Not surprisingly, there are a few blog directories that are a lot more important than the others. Among them, I would include Technorati.com, BlogCatalog.com and MyBlogLog.com.

While Technorati is not really a blog directory, it's a major player in the blogosphere and you should begin your journey by getting listed there.

The other two are both online communities where you can accumulate friends and communicate with other bloggers. There are people who focus all their marketing efforts within these communities, proving that their participation alone can drive more traffic to their blogs.

There are a lot of services to get your blog registered with all the major directories for a fee. These fees range from $2 to $200 and I have listed a couple on the Tactical Execution website.

**Tactical Execution > Resources > Useful Links
> Blog Resource Links**

Building a blog is like building a house. You have to start with the foundation. Most bloggers start their blog by installing double-pain windows and decorative planters. Don't fall into that trap. Start with the foundation. Get your blog listed on all the major directories. After that, there's a long list of things you can do and we'll go through a number of them in the coming chapters.

Step-by-step action guide:

- [ ] *Optimize your blog title and description.*
- [ ] *Register your blog at <u>Technorati.com</u>.*
- [ ] *Register your blog at <u>BlogCatalog.com</u>.*
- [ ] *Register your blog at <u>MyBlogLog.com</u>.*
- [ ] *Review the blog links on Tactical Execution.*
- [ ] *Consider using a service to get listed.*
- [ ] *Announce to the internet that you exist!*

Blog Directories

24

Outbound Links = Currency

Outbound Links = Currency

This may be the most important reality behind effective blogging. Without this, your blog's popularity will grow far slower then it could otherwise.

You have to understand that all the other bloggers are looking for the same thing you are. They're looking for traffic. They're looking for an audience. They're looking for exposure.

The second thing you need to understand is that modern marketing is built on an abundance mentality, and not a scarcity mentality. The days of keeping your ideas secret and working only to benefit yourself are over. That type of blatant self-interest does far more to harm your business than grow it.

Help others. Endorse others. Provide value to your audience. Whenever you find something valuable (even if it's on a competitor's website), link to it and tell your audience all about it. Become a beacon of value for your followers.

You want your blog to be a single gateway to the entire universe of resources in your field. You want the world to know that they can visit *your* blog and immediately have access to every possible resource they might need to help them achieve their objective.

Value leads to trust. Trust leads to sales. People need to trust you first and only then will they buy your product. By providing value, you're building trust. And how can you build value on your blog? There are two ways.

First, you can deliver outstanding content yourself. You can write good stuff. Second, you can endorse other people's content by linking out to it. If you find something useful on someone else's blog or website, blog about it and include a link.

Now, let's look at this from the other side. Do you think the bloggers you link to will appreciate your endorsement? By providing a link, you're even willing to divert some of *your* traffic to *their* website. Do you think they'll appreciate it? Of course they will. That's exactly what they're looking for. You're helping them out.

It's easy to see who's linking to your blog. You can usually find out right through your blogging administrative dashboard, not to mention Google and Technorati.

So, when these bloggers see that you linked to them, what do you think they'll do?

If it were me, I would check out your blog and see what you wrote about me. Right? I'd be curious. Wouldn't you? Absolutely. That means the majority of bloggers you link to will visit *your* blog and see what you're up to. And if they like what you're doing, they might just link back.

That's precisely my point.

By linking to other bloggers, you increase the odds they'll link back to you. At the very least, they'll know you exist.

And while you may not control who links to your blog, you certainly control who you link to. In fact, you can link to the most popular blogs in your field! We'll be talking about that in the next chapter.

Blogging is a human activity. By endorsing someone else, you accumulate brownie points. You get in the good graces of your peers. That's where you want to be. Give love, get love. You should link out to as many different blogs and websites as you possibly can. It helps you get completely interwoven in the blogosphere.

Imagine receiving an email from a fellow blogger who wrote a post all about you and your blog. How would that feel? It would make you happy, wouldn't it?

You can be that fellow blogger. You can make someone feel like that. You have the power. Use it.

Step-by-step action guide:

☐ *Abandon the scarcity mentality.*
☐ *Adopt the abundance mentality.*
☐ *Push value out to your audience.*
☐ *Link to every resource you possibly can.*
☐ *Send emails to those you link to.*
☐ *Avoid criticizing. Give love to get love.*

Outbound Links = Currency

25

Subscribe to Top Bloggers

Who are the top bloggers in your field?

In Chapter 24, we discussed the opportunity you have to link out to other bloggers as a way of gaining exposure and building your link structure. Some people hate the idea of that because they see it as a direct endorsement of their biggest competitors.

If you feel that way, change your mind!!

The abundance mentality will win in the future. It's already winning. The very first thing you should do as a blogger is identify the top players in your field. Who's the very best? Who do you respect? Who has the biggest audience? Once identified, you should literally trip over yourself trying to publicly endorse their work.

Your willingness to reference these industry leaders directly and link to their resources immediately increases your own stature. You look like a peer rather than an adoring fan. It makes you look like a leader yourself.

I highly recommend identifying and subscribing to the top bloggers in your field. Technorati is a great place to find them. So is Google BlogSearch. For me, it includes people like Seth Godin, John Reese, Frank Kern, David Bass, Perry Belcher, Bob Bly and Dan Kennedy, among others. Find the leaders in *your* field and subscribe to their feeds.

By the way, the easiest way to subscribe to these feeds is to use a 'reader' like Google Reader. Most of them are free and provide a great way to follow the latest posts all in one place. When you log on, they provide a list of all the posts published by those you're following, just like a newspaper. You can then scroll through and see what everybody's blogging about.

It's also worth mentioning that most of these 'readers' let you search for feeds using keywords or a person's name and then sort the results by the number of subscribers. Although the internet is full of hidden treasures, it's a pretty safe bet that the gurus in your field already have large followings, making them easy to find.

Once you've identified your industry leaders and subscribed to their feeds using a reader, I recommend checking the latest posts every time you write a post yourself. Get in the habit. By doing so, your awareness skyrockets and you will almost always have other blogs you can link to in your post.

This is such a simple strategy but you'd be amazed how few people take advantage of it. I'm guilty of it myself. Sometimes, I just don't feel like I have the time but I'm always sorry when I skip the step.

I describe the people I follow as "thought leaders". They're usually on the cutting edge of my field: internet marketing. They know what's hot in the market. And reading their posts allows me to stay up-to-date on the latest strategies and add my own contribution to the discussion.

If your post addresses the hottest topic in your field, you'll be perfectly positioned to capture some of the browsers searching for those keywords on search engines. And if your posts link out to other leaders in your field, your audience will start to grow. Finally, if some of those "thought leaders" start linking back to you, your exposure could explode quickly.

Surround yourself with leaders. Surround yourself with top quality content. It improves all aspects of your game and your audience benefits as well.

Step-by-step action guide:

- ☐ *Select keywords to describe your field.*
- ☐ *Visit Technorati and find the top bloggers.*
- ☐ *Use Google Blogsearch to find others.*
- ☐ *Subscribe to the top bloggers in your field.*
- ☐ *Select a 'reader' like Google Reader.*
- ☐ *Add all your feeds to your reader.*
- ☐ *Always check your reader before writing.*
- ☐ *Follow the "hot" topics and discussion.*
- ☐ *Link to others writing about the same topic.*

Subscribe to Top Bloggers

26

Social Bookmarking

What is social bookmarking?

You might recognize names like Digg, Delicious, Reddit and StumbleUpon – or not! Either way, these platforms are playing an important role in the social media explosion revolutionizing today's internet.

Here's how they work. We're all familiar with favorites. When you visit a site you like, you can bookmark it to your favorites, allowing you to quickly find it again in the future. But what happens when you're using someone else's computer? You don't have access to your favorites anymore because they're on *your* computer, not theirs.

Social bookmarking platforms are websites where you can create an account for yourself and then bookmark your favorites to that account *rather* than your computer. That means you'd have access to your favorites from any computer in the world.

That's pretty neat, but it's a fairly basic piece of functionality. But wait! There's more.

The cool thing is that the social bookmarking platforms aggregate all the bookmarking activity of their users. Some of these platforms have over 20 million users! That means you could go to Digg and search for tags like 'sports' or 'news' and find the most bookmarked websites in the world about those topics, not according to some complicated search engine algorithm but according to your *peer group*.

You could also search for "fly fishing in Alaska" or "sonatas by Mozart" or "mating habits of mosquitoes". In each case, you'll find the information your peer group is endorsing. The important part is your *peer group* is guiding your search, not a search engine.

That's a huge opportunity. That allows the peer group to educate itself. It allows the peer group to evaluate content and reward content they like. It allows *you* to write a blog post and then bookmark it on the social bookmarking platforms, allowing your peer group to evaluate it for themselves. If they like it, their validation could catapult your post to a global audience within a few hours!

Every single day, blog posts get to the front page of Digg. Every day, someone's content is endorsed by the peer group, driving it up the rankings until it's at the very top. And every day, the posts that get to the top receive literally millions of visitors from around the world.

Is it easy to get to the top of Digg? No, it's not. But is it possible? Yes.

The technology driving social bookmarking platforms delivers real-time democracy for users. It's changing the way people think. Back in the good old days, people looked at the *source* first and the *content* second. Today, that is completely reversed. Today, people look at the *content* first and the *source* second.

That means good quality content wins, even if it comes from a no-name blogger. If it's good quality content, it's good quality content. That's it. You don't need a fancy title or impressive credentials. All you need is good quality content. And that represents an opportunity for all of us.

This same cultural shift allowed an unknown community organizer to become President of the United States in eight short years. Think about it.

Pick your specialty. Stake your claim. Own your little piece of our information economy and demonstrate your expertise. If you provide real value with good quality content, and if your content is validated by your peer group, the real-time democracy of today's social internet will take care of the rest.

When creating your blog, be sure to include all the social bookmarking buttons right on your website. Doing so reminds your readers to bookmark the page if they like it, and it's easier too. And when you publish a new post, make sure it gets bookmarked on the major platforms, even if you have to do it yourself.

Once it's listed on those platforms, you pass the baton to your peer group and give the power to them. If your post provides real value, you never know where it might end up.

Step-by-step action guide:

- [ ] *Visit DIGG, Delicious and StumbleUpon.*
- [ ] *Search for your keywords on each platform.*
- [ ] *Notice which posts come up at the top.*
- [ ] *Create an account for yourself on each.*
- [ ] *Watch what other users bookmark.*
- [ ] *Connect with others you agree with.*
- [ ] *Ensure your blog posts get bookmarked.*

Social Bookmarking

27

Blog Carnivals

Would you like your work to be featured in a magazine?

Anyone looking to build exposure for themselves or their business would jump at the opportunity. Not only would it demonstrate your expertise in front of a whole new audience, but it would also give you tremendous credibility in front of your own.

What's a Blog Carnival?

A Carnival is just like a magazine except that it's online. Certain bloggers host Carnivals about one topic or another and *you* can submit your blog posts to be included. If the hosting blogger agrees to feature your post, the Carnival will introduce your contribution and include a link for interested readers to read your post ... on your blog.

Turns out, there's a great place to see all the Carnivals taking place and submit your posts to those whose topic relates to your content.

http://BlogCarnival.com/

This platform allows those *hosting* Carnivals and those *contributing* to Carnivals to connect with each other. All the upcoming Carnivals are listed and categorized, making them easy to identify. You can then submit your work directly to the host.

I do this once every couple of weeks. In less than an hour, I can scan the upcoming Carnivals and submit my new posts to 20 or 30 different Carnivals. Obviously, your acceptance rate depends on the quality of your work but I generally get accepted by at least half the Carnivals I submit to.

That means I receive 10 or 15 new one-way inbound links to my blog every two weeks. Not only does that fuel my Google ranking but it also adds to my Technorati authority, not to mention all the traffic that finds my blog from Carnivals hosted elsewhere on the internet.

As you probably guessed, the second major opportunity lies with hosting a Carnival yourself. On BlogCarnival.com, it's very easy to set up your own Carnival and let other bloggers start submitting posts to *you*. You can select those you like and include them into your own Carnival. In short order, you'll become a known quantity among the most active bloggers in your field.

BlogCarnival.com goes a step further, offering their InstaCarnival feature that provides basic HTML code to literally cut and paste into your blog. That means it would take you no more than five minutes to publish each edition of your Carnival. It couldn't be any easier than it already is. Take advantage of it.

Blog Carnivals represent an active ongoing conversation in the blogosphere; a conversation you can participate in. We'll be talking about this more in Chapter 28 but the point is that your participation is all that's required to get known in your area. You can quickly get known as an active contributor in your area of expertise and that can leave you with enhanced credibility within your peer group.

This is the last chapter about effective blogging. We started by discussing the importance of outbound links and how they can encourage others to link back to you. We discussed top bloggers and how you can benefit by subscribing to their blogs. We discussed the Social Bookmarking platforms and how you can use them to announce your work to your peer group. And in this chapter, we introduced Blog Carnivals as a fantastic way to become tightly integrated into the blogosphere.

This is powerful stuff. Done consistently, you can change your business (and your life) forever.

Step-by-step action guide:

- [ ] *Visit BlogCarnival.com.*
- [ ] *Search the upcoming carnival listings.*
- [ ] *Find appropriate carnivals for your posts.*
- [ ] *Create an account for yourself.*
- [ ] *Submit recent posts with a description.*
- [ ] *Consider hosting your own blog carnival.*
- [ ] *Click "Organize new carnival."*
- [ ] *Schedule a new edition for your carnival.*
- [ ] *Watch the submissions come in. It's fun!*

Blog Carnivals

28

Conversations are Markets

How can you access a *market* on today's social internet?

I get asked this question all the time. And whether you realize it or not, we've been talking about it throughout this book. It all boils down to one simple idea. If you focus on this one concept, the rest takes care of itself.

Conversations are Markets.

If you want to access a particular market, you need to participate in the conversation surrounding that market. By participating in the conversation, you're engaging that community and becoming known within it. As a known quantity, members of that community become more open to your product or service.

By linking to other bloggers and content providers (Chapter 24), you are engaging in the conversation. Those other bloggers will see that you *exist*. And they will start to be aware of your thoughts and insights.

By subscribing to other top bloggers in your field (Chapter 25), you will stay current with the conversation in your field. Knowing what these thought-leaders are blogging about will give you an opportunity to chime in with your own perspective and expertise.

By sharing your posts on the social bookmarking platforms (Chapter 26), you're giving the world an opportunity to evaluate your content for themselves. If your content is good, it will be shared and distributed, making your contribution known within your community.

And by submitting your posts to blog carnivals (Chapter 27), you are once again engaging your community and contributing to the conversation.

But there's an even bigger opportunity.

Not only can you participate in the conversation, but you can actually *facilitate* that conversation as well. Think about the people who built any of the large forums or bulletin boards on the internet. Those people gain credibility by facilitating the conversation.

Think about the people who built Facebook or Digg or Twitter. Think about Barack Obama whose campaign built a platform that hosted the blogs of over 60,000 supporters. Whether you like him or not, Obama was facilitating an enormous conversation, and he benefited as a result.

In Chapter 27, we discussed Blog Carnivals. As we discussed, you can easily submit your blog posts to carnivals in your field. But you can do more than that. You can host your own carnivals and have other bloggers submit their posts to you.

Hosting your own carnival is a great simple way to begin facilitating the conversation in your field. All the active bloggers will quickly know you exist if you have your own carnival that you publish regularly.

Installing a forum on your blog is another strategy. There are open source options in this area including Simple Machines and others. If you have a substantial audience, a forum can quickly bring your online identity to the next level.

And of course, the standard blog functionality of allowing comments on your blog is another strategy to encourage the conversation. In fact, posting comments on other people's blogs is a great way to drive traffic to your website. We'll talk about that in Chapter 52.

People sometimes ask me if they should edit or delete derogatory comments on their blog. My answer is simple. Unless the comment is either spam or intentionally malicious, I would leave it up. Controversial comments are the best ones. They show you're being completely transparent. They prove you're authentic. And they encourage further dialog among your followers.

Any opportunity to encourage interaction and communication between your users is good. And if the thought-leaders in your field start participating as well, your traffic could explode quickly.

Conversations are markets. If you want to access a market on today's social internet, participate in and facilitate conversations. If you engage your community in an authentic way, you'll be amazed at the response you'll get.

Step-by-step action guide:

☐ *Find the conversation in your field.*
☐ *Actively participate in the conversation.*
☐ *Facilitate the conversation if possible.*
☐ *Encourage the conversation to continue.*
☐ *Negative comments are not always bad.*
☐ *Authentic interactions build credibility.*

Conversations are Markets

29

Leverage Facebook

Are you on Facebook yet?

If not, it's time to step up. No more avoidance strategies.
No more justifications. Facebook is here to stay and you
can use it to build your business ... and that's why we're
here. So let's get started.

First things first. This chapter is about Facebook and the
next chapter is about LinkedIn. You need to be on both.
So figure out your rules now. Decide who you want to *be*
on each platform and decide who you're willing to connect
and interact with.

One of the nicest things about Facebook is that you can
split your 'friends' up into groups and have different privacy
settings for each group. That means you can connect with
anyone you want and then restrict access to those who are
outside your circle of close friends.

But even with that functionality, Facebook and LinkedIn are
very different. You have the choice to decide what you
want to reveal on each platform. So take this opportunity
and make your rules. I don't care what they are but you
need to make them *before* you get started.

In this chapter, we focus on four primary opportunities on Facebook. There are others but these represent the most obvious places to start.

Facebook Pages. As you might know, your Facebook *profile* is restricted to those who are logged in. You can't just visit someone's profile unless you have a Facebook profile yourself. Furthermore, you can't see their full profile unless you're already connected as 'friends'.

Facebook *Pages* are different. They are publicly accessible. Not only that but they're also very powerful. You could literally use a Facebook Page as your primary website. So if you have a business, have your personal profile on Facebook and then build a Facebook Page for your business.

On your Facebook Page, you can add information about your business, links to your independent website (if you have one), images or logos, videos and a discussion board for your 'fans'. Yeah, that's right. Fans. People can become fans of your Facebook Page. Powerful.

The cool thing about this type of activity is that it's picked up on the news feed. In other words, if you 'became a fan' of my Facebook Page, your whole network of friends would be notified. They're also notified if you post something on the discussion board of my Facebook Page or if you RSVP to an event posted on my Facebook Page.

This is an incredible viral opportunity. By engaging people in your Facebook Page, you are augmenting your exposure through the personal networks of all your fans.

So how can you take advantage of that? You can start by creating a page that lots of people would want to be a fan of. Don't think about what would benefit *you*. Think about what would benefit your prospective fans.

Post events. That's the second major opportunity on Facebook. Post events that anyone would want to attend. Create a Facebook Page first and then post no-brainer events that anyone would want to go to. Fun free events.

This is not the place to charge lots of money. This is the place to give stuff away for free. You want everyone to RSVP to your event. Because if they do, all those RSVPs will be included in the news feeds of those people's networks and that could quickly expand your audience.

Pay-per-click (PPC) advertising. The third opportunity is the Facebook pay-per-click (PPC) advertising program. We'll be talking about Google PPC advertising in Chapter 56 but Facebook is a different animal all together.

For starters, there's very little competition for the Facebook PPC option. Second, you can precision target your audience. Third, if you point to a Facebook Page, the cost is even lower. All told, it's one of the best deals in town.

Tactical Execution has a round logo that you can find on the back cover of this book. I recently did a Facebook campaign and included an image of that logo in my ad. Over the course of a single week, I had over 63,000 impressions and it only cost me $29.

Now, just to be clear, I did *not* get 63,000 clicks. I only got about 100 clicks. But that's precisely the point. I only had to pay for 100 clicks but 63,000 people saw my Tactical Execution logo. That's great branding. Meanwhile, I only had to pay for the people who were actually interested in my event – money well spent.

Tagging Photos. The fourth opportunity is uploading photos and tagging the people in them. When you tag someone in a photo on Facebook, their network of friends is notified. Also, that photo then shows up in their profile forever (unless they untag themselves).

When you visit someone's profile, what do you do first? Quite often, you look at their photos. It's superficial but true. That represents another great opportunity.

Any time you hold events, take photos and post them to your Facebook Page. You can create a separate album for each event and include photos of the people in attendance. Try to include some signage of your business in the photo and then tag the people photographed.

Tagging photos on Facebook is a great viral mechanism that can help you spread the word about your business.

Create a Facebook Page. Post a great event. Promote the event using the Facebook PPC program and photograph and tag everyone who attends. Put it all together and Facebook can play a major role in your business' marketing program.

Step-by-step action guide:

- ☐ Create a free profile on Facebook.
- ☐ Configure your privacy settings.
- ☐ Create a Facebook Page for your business.
- ☐ Invite your network to become 'fans'.
- ☐ Encourage use of the discussion board.
- ☐ Post free and fun events to your Page.
- ☐ Advertise your events using PPC ads.
- ☐ Take photos of people at your events.
- ☐ Tag the people in each of the photos.
- ☐ Create photo albums on your Page.
- ☐ Be active, stay active and watch it grow.

Leverage Facebook

30

Leverage LinkedIn

How can you market yourself on LinkedIn?

Just like Facebook (Chapter 29), there are tricks that can make LinkedIn a powerful marketing tool. First, a bit of background.

LinkedIn is another social network that prides itself on being the most professional of the bunch. If there was a continuum of social networks from the least professional to the most professional, MySpace would probably be on the least professional side (although that is changing) while LinkedIn would be on the most professional. Facebook is somewhere in the middle.

As with most of these strategies, there are people who focus 100% of their marketing strategies *just* on LinkedIn. You could do the same thing. LinkedIn offers tremendous opportunities to those who know how to leverage it. Let's make sure you're in that group!

This chapter focuses on three opportunities on LinkedIn and there are more being introduced in the months ahead. LinkedIn has announced an aggressive plan to add business applications for its users. Let's start with a simple but powerful opportunity.

Blog integration. You can now integrate your blog with your LinkedIn profile so that your efforts to update your blog with valuable content automatically populate your LinkedIn profile as well.

This simple integration does a lot to show your LinkedIn network what you're up to. It also gives them an opportunity to see the topics you blog about and the value you provide for your audience.

Recommendations. The second opportunity is with recommendations. When you visit someone's profile on LinkedIn, what's the first thing you do. Again, it depends from person to person but many people read the recommendations first. It's the most fun.

Reading what a third party wrote about your friend or colleague is always interesting. Those recommendations are a goldmine. Go through your contacts and write recommendations for anyone you possibly can. By doing so, you augment your network by having a presence on the profile pages of your contacts.

Obviously, your recommendations have to be authentic. I absolutely do *not* endorse recommendations that are written for the sole purpose of gaining exposure. But if you have something good to say about someone in your network, do it. You'll kill two birds with one stone.

There's a third advantage as well. By recommending someone in your network, you're giving that person an incentive to recommend you back. If you wrote recommendations for 20 people in your network and half of them recommended you back, you would end up with 10 recommendations on your profile.

This may seem simple but you'd be surprised at the difference it makes. Similar to blogging, give love to get love. Your recommendations make you a more active member of the community and the recommendations on your profile leave you with more credibility for your own audience.

Answer questions. The third opportunity is with LinkedIn Answers, an area of the platform where people can ask questions or provide answers to other people's questions. Also, users can vote on the best answer for any given question, giving peer validation and credibility to valuable contributors.

The most active 'experts' on LinkedIn answer about 150 questions each week. That might seem like a lot but I guarantee those people are feeding their businesses by doing so. It's probably their primary marketing vehicle.

Let's run the numbers. If it takes five minutes to answer a question, 150 questions would take 750 minutes. If you did that in five business days, we're talking about 150 minutes each day; two and a half hours.

You don't need to be the most active to get noticed. Even if you only answer 10 questions each week, your answers will inevitably be seen by precisely those people who want that information. It's a great way to demonstrate your expertise directly to your target market.

The beauty with answering questions is it demonstrates your expertise beyond your circle of immediate contacts. Your contributions are seen throughout your network. And if your answers are frequently voted the best, your credibility will soar within the LinkedIn audience.

Applications. Get in the habit of clicking on Applications when on LinkedIn. As I mentioned, they have ambitious plans to add new applications and this is where they show up. The last time I checked, they had a Twitter application called Company Buzz. I'm sure there's more coming and I encourage you to stay on top of it.

Step-by-step action guide:

- ☐ *Create a free profile on LinkedIn.*
- ☐ *Include your full employment history.*
- ☐ *Click Applications to integrate your blog.*
- ☐ *Write recommendations for your contacts.*
- ☐ *Click Answers to see how that works.*
- ☐ *Search for your favorite keywords.*
- ☐ *Answer questions you know answers to.*
- ☐ *Check Applications regularly for new stuff.*

Leverage LinkedIn

31

Leverage Twitter

What the heck is Twitter??

Yes, it's true. Twitter has caused quite a stir in recent months. So we really can't dissect the social media topic without addressing Twitter and how to use it properly.

Fact is; Twitter has sparked a whole new vernacular. Those who use Twitter are called tweople and the things they post are called tweets. Let's break it down.

Twitter is a micro-blogging platform. That means you can post content, just like a traditional blog. The difference is that you only have 140 characters to work with. That's about two sentences, depending on your wording.

The idea behind Twitter is to answer the question: what are you doing? And people (or "tweople") post all sorts of short little tidbits about their lives.

Let's understand the logistics. Twitter is an online platform and you create your account there. When you post something, it shows up in your account on the Twitter.

You can subscribe to (or "follow") other people's tweets, so their posts automatically get pushed to your account. Other people can also follow *your* tweets. That means anything you write automatically gets pushed to them.

As basic as this may sound, Twitter has become a cultural phenomena. Some people are being followed by literally thousands of people and everyone who's anyone seems to be using the platform.

The primary appeal of Twitter is that you can get a tiny glimpse into the lives of other people … in real time! For example, I follow Chris Cillizza who tweets live from the White House briefing room. I follow a handful of internet marketing gurus and see what they're up to. I follow Al Gore and Lance Armstrong. And of course, I follow friends and colleagues who are in my personal network.

Because the act of 'following' someone is such a low-commitment decision, Twitter might be the easiest place to build an 'opt-in' list. If you're active on Twitter, you quickly get noticed and people will start following your tweets.

Once you have a big list of followers, your little bite-sized tweets start having a real impact. People respond to your tweets and visit the URLs you share. The whole thing can be incredibly powerful.

The fact remains that most people have absolutely no idea how to use Twitter so here are a few guidelines. There are really four reasons to write a tweet.

Community. Connect with the people you are following. Reply to their tweets and participate in their conversation. If someone replies to one of your tweets, be sure to acknowledge it by replying back to them.

Business. Tell your followers about *your* products and the benefits they offer. Provide resources and content that educate your audience about your business.

Wisdom. Tell your followers about *other* people's products and why you endorse them. Provide useful information and resources that can (hopefully) benefit their lives.

Personal. Invite your followers into your life and share some of your daily activities. Be authentic. Be real. People want to know who you are, not just your business.

There's an entire industry of tools being created for the growing Twitter population. Here are a few.

Search your keywords to find the conversation in your field.
http://search.twitter.com/

Group and manage your followers right on your desktop.
http://www.tweetdeck.com/

Create fancy background images for your Twitter profile.
http://www.twitbacks.com/

By the way, "hashtags" are an easy way to add searchable tags to your tweets by adding the # symbol before a given word. The Twitter hashtag for this book is #webify.

Step-by-step action guide:

- [ ] *Create a free account on Twitter.*
- [ ] *Find and follow gurus in your field.*
- [ ] *Invite your friends to follow you.*
- [ ] *Community – connect with your followers.*
- [ ] *Business – promote your products.*
- [ ] *Wisdom – promote other people's products.*
- [ ] *Personal – share a bit of your personal life.*
- [ ] *Pimp your account with related resources.*

Leverage Twitter

32

Social Media Mantras

Content is KING ... *or is it?*

This is a very common phrase on the internet. And in years gone by, it was very true. The single most important ingredient for online success was good quality content.

Today, with the social media revolution in full effect, I no longer agree with that statement. To me ...

Content is ... QUEEN.

So what took its place? What's now in the top spot?

Community Engagement.

Community engagement is KING. There is a very clear reason why this is true. Here goes. Bad quality content combined with community engagement beats good quality content by itself.

| **Bad Content** | **+** | **Community Engagement** | **>** | **Good Content** |

Now, if you have good quality content *and* community engagement, you win. No question. But even bad quality content can find an audience with effective community engagement.

So what is community engagement? It's your participation in the conversation. It's what we've been talking about for the past nine chapters. When you make a contribution to your community without trying to sell a product, you are engaging your community. You are participating in the conversation.

When you link to valuable resources on your blog, you are engaging your community.

When you submit your blog posts to the sites like DIGG, Delicious and StumbleUpon, you are engaging your community.

When you participate or host blog carnivals, you are engaging your community.

When you invite people to become fans of your new Facebook Page or attend one of your events, you are engaging your community.

When you recommend colleagues on LinkedIn or answer questions, you are engaging your community.

When you follow and are followed on Twitter, you are engaging your community. And by the way, when I offer a Twitter hashtag (#webify) for this book, I'm engaging *my* community as well and encouraging the conversation about my product.

Community engagement is the essence of the modern internet. Community engagement is at the center of the social media revolution. Conversations are Markets – same thing. Embrace this mantra and your journey on the internet will be far more productive.

So, community engagement is KING. Content is QUEEN. What's in third place?

Authenticity and Transparency.

Being authentic and transparent are critical. For better or for worse, the days of secrets are behind us. As soon as you try to put a spin on something, your audience will drop you like a rock. If you're caught in a lie, you're finished.

The best thing you can do today is freely admit your weaknesses and your failures. People are people. We all have shortcomings. Strive to be flawed. Perfection is passé.

What do you think when you see a perfectly produced video? You probably assume it was done by a professional marketing company. And as enjoyable as it might be to watch, you probably trust it less than an amateur-looking alternative of a real person with a real message.

Authenticity makes you a person, not a business. And transparency adds credibility to your message. Adopt these mantras and your actions will speak to the masses. Ignore them and your message will fall flat.

Step-by-step action guide:

- ☐ *Community Engagement is KING.*
- ☐ *Good quality content is QUEEN.*
- ☐ *Authenticity & Transparency comes in third.*
- ☐ *Participate in the conversation.*
- ☐ *Always provide value to your audience.*
- ☐ *Be a person first and a business second.*

Social Media Mantras

33

Social Media Integration

I don't have the time to do all this internet stuff!!

It's usually about this time that people start throwing their hands in the air. If you started at the beginning, you've gone through 32 chapters so far. We've discussed a lot of different things. How are you supposed to do all these new activities when you're far too busy already?!

Fear not.

Indeed, there are a lot of different platforms that all represent opportunities for you to build credibility and gain exposure online, but that doesn't mean you need to spend hours on each one. Turns out, one of the biggest trends of our day is *integration*.

Many of these social media platforms integrate easily with each other. And once integrated, your activity on one is automatically announced on the others. That means you could do something on *one* platform and have four or five different audiences populated all at the same time!

If you haven't already done so, create a Twitter account. Don't worry. It won't cost you anything. And while you're at it, open an Utterli account as well. Then open an account on YouTube and Flickr. And don't forget Facebook and LinkedIn.

These are all free platforms and they all integrate beautifully with each other. Let me give you an example.

I frequently use my cell phone to record audio messages to my Utterli account. When I do, it automatically populates my Twitter account. Twitter populates my Facebook profile. Twitter also populates my WordPress blog with a post announcing that I recorded an 'utter'. Utterli populates a widget I have on the sidebar of my blog and my blog populates my Facebook as well as my LinkedIn profile.

Wow! So that means one cell phone call (that usually takes me less than one minute to record) populates five audiences all at one time. Now that's efficiency! We all have cell phones. We all one minute each day when we can push some value out to our respective audiences. We just need to set up the infrastructure so we can do it as easily as possible.

I've written a lot of posts about Twitter and Utterli (formerly Utterz) on my blog. I also wrote a post all about social media integration. If you want more detailed information, you can find it on my blog.

Tactical Execution > Blog

We talked about Twitter in Chapter 31 but one of my favorite benefits (which I didn't mention in that chapter) is that Twitter has a very flexible API, meaning it integrates easily with a lot of different platforms.

It's worth noting that YouTube integrates nicely with Facebook and so do most other prominent social media platforms. As we mentioned in Chapter 30, LinkedIn is adding more all the time.

The point of this chapter is to encourage you to leverage these platforms and to do so in the most efficient way possible. They're extremely powerful and don't cost anything to try. So what's the harm? Sign up for an account and give it a shot.

Different people use the internet in different ways. Some like blogs. Some like videos or photos. Some like audio recordings. And some just spend time on social networks. Find ways to tie them all together so your contributions are automatically distributed to all of them.

Multi-platform integration is at the center of the buzz these days. You'll see more and more of this as the months drift by. Get started now so you can ride the wave that's driving the internet into the future.

Step-by-step action guide:

- ☐ *Push Twitter to your Facebook profile.*
- ☐ *Twitter also pushes to WordPress blogs.*
- ☐ *Push Utterli to your Twitter account.*
- ☐ *Push your blog to Facebook & LinkedIn.*
- ☐ *Push YouTube to your Facebook profile.*
- ☐ *Push Meetup to your Facebook profile.*
- ☐ *Always look for more integration features.*

Social Media Integration

34

Google Analytics

Who's visiting your website? Any idea??

This question lies at the heart of online success. You can only improve what you measure. But before we get into it, I need to explain something to you - something incredibly important.

There are no secrets on the internet.

Simple, but powerful. On the internet, everything can be tracked. If you're curious what people are searching for, you can find out. If you're curious which products are selling the best, you can find out. If you want to know where people are coming from and where they're going, you can find out.

The process of measuring all this online activity is called website analytics, and *everything* on the internet can be tracked. Turns out, you can access some amazingly powerful tools without spending a penny ... enter Google Analytics, stage left.

> http://www.google.com/analytics/

Let's break it down. Using Google Analytics, you can see:

☐   How many people are visiting your website.
☐   The keywords they used to find you on search engines.
☐   Which website referred them to you.
☐   What page they saw first.
☐   How much time they spent on your site.
☐   How many pages they visited.
☐   What page they left your site from.
☐   The geographic location of your visitors.
☐   The browser they're using.
☐   And a host of other facts, figures and statistics!

Installing Google Analytics is simple and free. Once you sign up for an account, the platform gives you a small piece of java script that you need to put into the footer of your website. Once complete, Google start tracking all the activity on your website.

It's impossible to over-state the importance of all this. You could track everything you do online and know with certainty what's working and what's not. There are no secrets. You can know without any shadow of a doubt. That's powerful stuff.

In the past, you would've had to do surveys or focus groups to gain insights to these topics. No longer. On the internet, you can see it all.

Let's take one example. Using Google Analytics, you can see your 'bounce rate'. That's the percentage of people who leave your website after viewing any particular page.

Now, just to be clear, you do *not* want people leaving your website. You want them to keep browsing. If they're leaving your site from one particular page, you need to improve that page to keep your visitors interested.

With Google Analytics, you could check all your pages and sort the results by the bounce rate. Then go down to the bottom of the list and you'll immediately see one of the weak links on your website; a page where a lot of people decided to leave your site.

Do this exercise once each month and try to improve the two or three worst pages from a bounce rate perspective. If you did that one simple task, you would be continually improving your site and keeping your audience engaged.

This is just one example but there are dozens. Google Analytics is an incredibly powerful platform and it gives you the opportunity to systematically improve your website.

There are a lot of other platforms that provide analytics data and some of them are very good. You're welcome to use whichever platform you like. I focused on Google Analytics in this chapter because it's free, powerful and extremely well used.

Step-by-step action guide:

- ☐ *Sign up for a Google Analytics account.*
- ☐ *Put the script into the footer of your site.*
- ☐ *Let the platform start accumulating data.*
- ☐ *Visit your analytics account regularly.*
- ☐ *Click on every option, explore everything.*
- ☐ *Monitor your absolute unique visitors.*
- ☐ *See which websites are referring visitors.*
- ☐ *Check the keywords that bring you traffic.*
- ☐ *Notice how long people stay on your site.*
- ☐ *Check which pages they go to the most.*
- ☐ *Never stop looking for more insights.*

Google Analytics

35

Understand Analytics Data

"My website gets 30,000 visitors per month!"

That's what this guy told me once, and he wasn't the first. People are always trying to impress me with the traffic their websites are supposedly getting. Maybe they do it to you too.

Turns out, you can find out a *lot* about someone's website all on your own. But before we get to that, let me explain a few important distinctions.

First, a 'hit' is *not* a 'visitor'. A hit is any click on any link on your website. If you have a bunch of links and someone visits your site and starts browsing around, they can easily rack up 20 or 30 hits during one visit.

Most people who claim their website is getting thousands of visitors are misreading their analytics. Those websites might be getting thousands of hits but far fewer visitors. In the case of the guy above, his website was getting about 1500 visitors per month - not bad but not great either.

Going a step further, a visitor is not the same as an 'absolute unique visitor'. If you visit your own website twice each day, you could be accounting for 50 or 60 visits (and 1000+ hits) each month. When reading your analytics, you want to see how many absolute unique visitors you're getting. That's the important number.

Here in the US, you can get a fairly good idea how many visitors a site is getting by checking its Alexa ranking. Alexa is the largest third party traffic monitoring site on the internet. With a few million people using their browser toolbar, they can estimate the traffic to different websites based on the browsing activity of their users.

In Europe and Asia, Alexa is less used so the traffic statistics are less reliable. But here in America, you can get a good idea how popular a given site is by checking on Alexa.

What does that mean? It means that you now have a tool at your disposal every time someone tries to impress you with their traffic statistics.

And why would that matter? Simple. Everyone's looking for affiliates, sponsors, advertisers and partners, and it's good to know which ones have real traffic and which ones are just blowing smoke.

The guy I told you about at the beginning wanted me to give him exclusive rights to sell my educational CDs. When he first proposed the idea, I considered it. But then I got back to my office and checked him out on Alexa. What a fraud. My site was getting more traffic than his!

By the way, a higher score on Alexa is *not* what you want. It's the lower scores that are good. For example, the number one website is the one with the *most* traffic. As of this writing, Yahoo is #1, Google is #2 and YouTube is #3.

Any website with an Alexa rank of 400,000 or less is probably getting at least 100 visitors per day. A site with rank of 1,000,000 is getting less than 50 visitors per day and a website with a rank higher than 2,000,000 is getting almost no traffic at all.

Here are a couple other tricks you should be aware of. When you go to Google, you can enter some codes to learn things about any given website.

| site:www.WebsiteName.com | **Search** |

This tells you how many pages are on the website.

| link:www.WebsiteName.com | **Search** |

This tells you the number of links pointing to the website.

You can also learn the Google PageRank of any particular website. The Google toolbar provides it or you could just type 'google pagerank checker' into Google to find tons of places where you can enter a URL and determine its Google PageRank.

The PageRank is important because it shows how relevant Google thinks a particular site is. The score ranges from 0 to 10 where 10 is the best. And believe it or not, a PageRank of four or higher is actually pretty good.

The PageRank score is calculated on a logarithmic scale so the move from three to four is big. The jump from four to five is even bigger and the scores higher than five are increasingly significant as you move up the ladder.

The point is that if a particular website has a Google PageRank of two or three, it's probably not getting a lot of organic traffic from search engines. Once the site has a PageRank of four or higher, it's probably coming up fairly high on organic Google searches and getting some respectable traffic as a result.

Between these four things (the Alexa ranking, the number of pages on the site, the number of inbound links and the Google PageRank score), you can get a pretty good idea about the significance of any particular website, including your own.

These are all little tricks you can use to become savvier as an internet user. Use them to evaluate your own progress and cut through all the hot air on today's internet!

Step-by-step action guide:

☐ *Check your Alexa traffic ranking.*
☐ *Check your number of pages on Google.*
☐ *Check your inbound links on Google.*
☐ *Check your Google PageRank score.*
☐ *Keep track of your progress over time.*
☐ *Check the statistics for your competitors.*
☐ *Verify claims made by big-talkers.*
☐ *Learn to monitor these statistics closely.*

Understand Analytics Data

36

Internet Directories

Are internet directories useless?

There was a time when you could accumulate valuable one-way inbound links by registering your website on a bunch of online directories. Those days are gone. The search engines no longer give much credence to directory links.

Are there exceptions? Absolutely. The DMOZ open directory project, for example, still offers a valuable link - and there are others. You can find a list of good ones on the Tactical Execution website:

**Tactical Execution > Resources > Useful Links
> Valuable Online Directories**

These directories are still worth getting registered on, but they're not the reason for this chapter.

There are more and more directories that list companies operating within one industry or another. Dentists. Chiropractors. Hauling companies. Real estate agents. Insurance brokers. Contractors. Salons. Whatever.

A single industry is often referred to as a vertical. Getting listed on directories within your vertical can be very valuable, primarily because prospective customers are finding these directories and using them like people once used the Yellow Pages.

In many cases, getting registered within these directories doesn't cost anything because the websites hosting them want to cultivate a complete list, making their directory more valuable and attracting more visitors as a result.

Go to Google and search for your keywords along with the word "directory". Browse through the first five or 10 pages and see what you can find. Within a single hour, you can probably find two or three directories – maybe more – and get your company listed along with a link to your website.

A few years ago, people registered with online directories to get inbound links. Today, the search engine algorithms have diminished that opportunity. But the more specific directories still offer value – not for search engines but for *humans*. Getting listed within niche directories can bring you customers.

Your local Chamber of Commerce is another example of a niche directory. Of course, membership in a Chamber of Commerce isn't free but their directories are specific to your location, making them more relevant to users.

Other community organizations like Rotary, Kiwanis and Lions have similar directories for their members. Check with the associations operating in your industry or clubs that cater to your profession. They all offer directories where your listing can attract qualified prospects.

Allocate a few hours to search for these directories and register with as many as you can. Make note of the ones that aren't free and prioritize your list for future consideration. Maybe you can afford to get listed with a few right away. Maybe not. Either way, these directories can play a major role in helping you establish your online identity.

In the next chapter, we'll be discussing some extremely important social media websites that you absolutely *must* be registered with. The internet marketing implications are big and immediate.

Step-by-step action guide:

☐ *Google your keywords plus "directory".*
☐ *Try to find directories within your vertical.*
☐ *Register your company on the free ones.*
☐ *Make note of those that aren't free.*
☐ *Register when your budget allows.*
☐ *Contact your local Chamber of Commerce.*
☐ *Find local Rotary, Kiwanis & Lions clubs.*
☐ *Determine the fee and member base.*
☐ *Check the prominence of their websites.*
☐ *Join if it would add to your online presence.*

Internet Directories

37

Online Branding

Want to be on page #1 of Google?

Stupid question. Of course you do! Turns out, there are some websites that can quickly put your company right on the first page for searches in your local community, even if you don't have a website! They include Yelp, CitySearch, Yahoo Local, MerchantCircle and Google Local among others.

Chapter 36 discussed niche directories that cater to specific verticals like your industry or even your geographic location. These directories can do an amazing job getting your name in front of qualified prospects, but they are less likely to show up on the front page of Google.

Yahoo Local, CitySearch and Yelp are different. They don't necessarily attract hordes of internet users who are all looking *only* for your particular service. On the contrary, they offer listings on a wide variety of topics, but they're such huge platforms that they tend to rank high on the search engines.

Here's the strategy. Visit all these websites and sign up for an account. By doing so, you're simply registering your existence in their database. Then, once your account is created, get some of your past clients to write reviews of your business on those platforms.

The best example is Yelp because they are specifically designed to capture reviews from the public. It's very easy to create an account and start accumulating reviews. Once you have a few (and hopefully they're all glowing), your existence on Yelp will start showing up in Google searches.

A client of mine was frustrated trying to get more clients online. We set up a Yelp account and had three of his past clients write testimonials for him. Now, when people search for his service (which is garbage removal) in his city, those Yelp reviews show up on the first page (while his own website is on page four or five).

In fact, of the 10 listings that come on the first page, he's mentioned in four of them! His listing on Yahoo Local comes up (listing #4) followed by MerchantCircle (listing #5), CitySearch (listing #7) and Yelp (listing #9).

Note that his own website is *not* listed on the first page, but his company dominates the top search results!

That's the opportunity these websites provide. They're such large platforms that they almost always come up near the top. Some are free. Others charge a fee but the online visibility is well worth the investment.

Yelp deserves a few more comments. While positive reviews are the inevitable goal, you want to be a bit careful about it. Getting reviews from people who aren't already active on Yelp looks suspicious and is sometimes referred to as "gaming" Yelp.

When asking past clients to write reviews for you, ask them if they are already using Yelp. If so, their review will definitely help you. If not, you're better off getting them to write reviews on other platforms like Yahoo Local or MerchantCircle. Leave Yelp to active Yelpers.

All of these websites allow you to leverage their impressive search engine rankings for your own benefit. Don't let that opportunity pass you by.

Most people believe the only way to show up on Google is to have an incredible website that is perfectly optimized for the search engines. That's not true. There are other ways – strategies that are more effective and less expensive than trying to build a huge website all on your own (or hiring someone else to do it).

The easiest way to find all the various platforms is to search for your industry keywords and look at the domain names at the bottom of each listing. By looking at the URL as well as the description text, you can usually identify the platforms that host profiles for other competitors.

To get you started, look for listings with Yelp, CitySearch or Yahoo in the URL. Those will give you a good idea of the usual structure, making it easy to find other websites you can target as well. I recommend doing this every month or so, just to make sure you've taken advantage of all the opportunities available in your industry.

These are simple strategies that only take a few hours to pursue. The best part is that you can easily see what your competition is doing, just by looking at the search results in your field. By consistently targeting all the platforms others are using, you'll quickly populate the internet with positive references of your business and that exposure can bring you the online customers you're looking for.

Another advantage is that these websites get indexed by Google regularly. That means you can start seeing results quickly. I recently created a page on MerchantCircle and found the listing on Google within 30 minutes.

Get started! Done properly, you can be on the first page of Google in short order.

Step-by-step action guide:

- ☐ *Create an account on Yahoo Local.*
- ☐ *Create an account on Google Local.*
- ☐ *Create an account on Yelp.*
- ☐ *Create an account on MerchantCircle.*
- ☐ *Consider an account on CitySearch ($$).*
- ☐ *Search for your keywords on Google.*
- ☐ *Look for other platforms others are using.*
- ☐ *Ask past clients to write reviews for you.*
- ☐ *Continue checking for new platforms.*

Online Branding

38

Categorize Your Content

What should you give away? What should you charge money for?

Marketing in the 21st century is all about demonstrating your expertise and providing value *before* asking for the sale. It's all about offering your audience a sample of your brilliance so they can experience your value. So what information do you have to give away for free?

This chapter is all about categorizing your content ... and it's one of the most important concepts in this entire book.

Before we get started, we have to define "content". I'm talking about your expertise. I'm talking about your knowledge. I'm talking about the things you know that other people *want* to know.

If you don't already have a particular expertise, you need to get one. You need to look out into the universe and pick your niche – pick the thing you're going to be an expert in. Even if you sell a product, you can be an expert in the uses of that product or the technology behind that product. Whatever you do, you need to stake your claim and become an authority on your topic.

We discussed this in Chapter 2.

Once you start accumulating content, break it down into three categories: beginner, intermediate and advanced. Every time you acquire new content, think of these categories and think about which category your new knowledge belongs in.

Here's the plan ...

In your effort to demonstrate your expertise and build trust with your audience, you're going to give the beginner content away for free. You can use it to build your website, write articles, create podcasts or record YouTube videos.

Give away the intermediate content as well but collect information about your audience in exchange for it. For example, you could ask for names and email addresses in exchange for a PDF white paper or a special report.

You could also get your audience to fill out a brief survey to receive the content. Either way, you want to use the intermediate content as a way of learning more about your audience. This information plays an important role in your future marketing strategies.

The advanced content is where you make some money. This is where you finally earn a profit. You could deliver this advanced content in the form of consulting jobs. You could create information products (like a big e-book or a bunch of CDs or DVDs) and sell them online. You could write a book or conduct training workshops. Whatever you choose, the advanced content is where you can finally put some cash in your pocket.

Keep in mind that the 'advanced' content could simply be the practical application of the intermediate content. A lot of people have access to great information but don't understand how to take action. That means your advanced content could involve detailed instructions for *using* your intermediate content.

List all the specific little topics you could address. Create the three categories and put each topic in the appropriate category. Pretend you're a teacher and treat your content as a series of lessons. That makes it easier to put the information into categories.

It's very important to get this concept right. Your internet marketing efforts depend on a content-rich website and strategic sampling of your expertise across the web. The next three chapters go into each category in more detail and provide some specific examples.

These strategies are powerful enough to form the foundation of a highly effective online marketing campaign. This is where the rubber hits the road. From now on, everything we do is designed to attract qualified prospects to your business!

Step-by-step action guide:

- [ ] *Pretend you're a teacher.*
- [ ] *Think about all the lessons you could offer.*
- [ ] *Create a detailed list of all these lessons.*
- [ ] *Add to the list any time you think of more.*
- [ ] *Identify all the beginner lessons (topics).*
- [ ] *Identify all the intermediate lessons.*
- [ ] *Identify all the advanced lessons.*
- [ ] *Split your list into three separate lists.*
- [ ] *Add new knowledge to the appropriate list.*
- [ ] *Learn to think along these categories.*

Categorize Your Content

39

Beginner Content = Trust

Leverage: create content once ... *and use it seven times!*

If you're smart about this, you can flood the internet with your expertise and work *less* than your competition.

In Chapter 38, we talked about categorizing your content into beginner, intermediate and advanced. The idea was to give the beginner content away in order to demonstrate your expertise and build trust with your audience.

Your website or blog is the perfect place for some of that content. Get the list of 'lessons' you put together and look through your beginner and intermediate topics. Let's start with the beginner topics. We'll get to the intermediate category in Chapter 40.

Take each beginner lesson and write an article about it. Always make sure your articles are at least 500 words long. If you write an article that's longer than 1500 words, break it into two separate articles. Are you ready? We'll be using your articles in seven different ways, maximizing the bang you get for your buck.

First, publish your article as a post on your blog. Easy.

Second, bookmark your new blog post on a few of the large social bookmarking sites like DIGG, Delicious and StumbleUpon.

Third, visit BlogCarnival.com and submit your new blog post to a bunch of upcoming blog carnivals.

Fourth, modify your article slightly and publish it on EzineArticles.com and some of the other article directories on the internet. You could even use a distribution platform like iSnare.com to get it on hundreds of different sites within a few days. We'll talk about this in Chapter 51.

Fifth, summarize your article into a punchy bullet-point PDF file and add a bunch of links to your website. Upload your new PDF to the many free e-book directories. You'll be amazed at how this one little strategy can deliver traffic to your website month after month.

Sixth, get a microphone ($50 or less), download Audacity (free software) and read your article into the mike. Save the recording as an MP3 file. Get an RSS hosting account ($5 per month) and create your own podcast. Upload your MP3 file and register the podcast with iTunes.

By the way, RSS stands for Really Simple Syndication. It's true. An RSS hosting account is an online place where you can upload your MP3 files, allowing people to download them from iTunes (or wherever). Here's who I use:

http://www.libsyn.com/

Seventh, get a FLIP digital video recorder (about $110) and explain your lesson into the camera. Don't worry. It doesn't have to be fancy. Just explain the concept like you were explaining it to a friend. Once you're done, add your website address to the video and upload it to YouTube.

By following these steps, you can take one piece of beginner content – one lesson – and use it in seven different formats, populating multiple platforms with your expertise. This is powerful stuff. It's extremely efficient and caters to the different ways people use the internet.

Don't make this more difficult than it needs to be. Most people think they need to create new content for every platform. No way! That's too much work. You could write one or two lessons each week and end up with a massive online identify within a few months.

Here's a sad reality. This chapter offers one of the most powerful strategies you could imagine, but most people reading it won't follow the advice.

If you could commit to just one thing, commit to this. If you follow these seven steps, you'll spend *less* time and get *better* results than 99% of your competition.

Step-by-step action guide:

- ☐ *Pick a topic and write a 500-word article.*
- ☐ *Post your article as a post on your blog.*
- ☐ *Submit it to the Social Bookmarking sites.*
- ☐ *Submit it to upcoming Blog Carnivals.*
- ☐ *Modify and publish it on article directories.*
- ☐ *Make it into a punchy how-to PDF e-book.*
- ☐ *Upload it to the free e-book directories.*
- ☐ *Read it into a microphone and save as MP3.*
- ☐ *Upload it to an RSS hosting account.*
- ☐ *Register it as a podcast on iTunes.*
- ☐ *Buy a FLIP recorder or a camcorder.*
- ☐ *Record yourself talking about the topic.*
- ☐ *Add your website address to the video.*
- ☐ *Upload the video to YouTube.*

Beginner Content = Trust

40

Intermediate Content = List

How many people are on your email list?

In Chapter 19, we spoke about building your email list. Have you started? How many people do you have so far?? Did you set up your autoresponder? I hope so. And maybe you already have hundreds or even thousands of people on that list. If so, congratulations!

This chapter discusses your intermediate content and how you can use it to gain more *information* about your audience. One of the most valuable pieces of information you can get is their email address. Once you have that, you can stay in touch with them far into the future.

Chapter 39 discussed leveraging your beginner content by using it in seven different ways on different platforms and catering to different audiences. That's one of the most powerful chapters in this book. Done properly, you can be more successful than 99% of your competition while working less. Sounds good to me!

But there's one thing we didn't discuss and it's just as important as leveraging your content.

Wherever you offer your free beginner content, you *must* tell your audience what else you offer (your intermediate and advanced content) and include a call-to-action so they know how to get it. Your beginner content demonstrates your expertise but your intermediate content is where your audience starts to interact with you. Your intermediate content is the beginning of your sales funnel.

Let's say you have a 17-page white paper as your intermediate content. Maybe it reveals new trends in your industry. Perhaps it lists the top tactics to find new clients, grow revenues or reduce costs. One great idea is to do a survey and then compile the results into a report.

At the bottom of your blog post, you should instruct your readers to click a link to receive the report. When publishing your articles, use the Author Resource Box to tell people about the report and provide a link. When uploading a free e-book, make sure it has links to the report. When you record your podcast, tell your listeners about it. And in your YouTube video, be sure to mention the report and tell them where to get it.

All of your beginner content should point to your intermediate content. You're building a sales funnel. You're leading your prospects down a path. First, you tease them with some great complimentary information – whet their appetite. Then, you entice them with more goodies – more valuable incentives – to take action and interact with you.

Soon, we'll be inviting them to spend money, but not yet. We still need to build trust. We want them to be *soooo* impressed that spending money with you is a complete no-brainer. We'll get to that in Chapter 41.

The important thing is that the people who take the next step need to give you some information before they can get the promised intermediate content. Although you could ask for just about anything, one of the best things to ask for is their email address. And an email autoresponder like Constant Contact or Aweber makes that easy to do.

As you know, most of this book is available for free as an email course on my Tactical Execution website. Those who subscribe get one email each week for a year, and it's all done automatically. I don't have to do a thing. The system automatically sends out the emails according to a predetermined time-lapse schedule. It's called an email autoresponder and I use Aweber, a leading provider.

http://www.aweber.com/

Within a few minutes, you can setup a simple sign-up form and put it on your website. Believe me; it's easy to do! Then, you can write the first email people receive when they sign up. You can also upload a PDF file and have Aweber attached it with the email. That means you can get Aweber to deliver a report or white paper (or whatever) all without having to lift a finger. Perfect.

What does this mean? It means you need to *create* your intermediate content first and then create a page on your website where people can enter their email address to *receive* your intermediate content. And finally, you need to include a call-to-action with every piece of beginner content you publish.

Whether you're using Constant Contact or Aweber or some other autoresponder, you can usually create as many lists as you want. If you already have an autoresponder set up, don't worry. Just create a separate list and a separate sign-up form and you'll start building a second list.

Some people will sign up for one or the other. Some will sign up for both. I have six different sign-up forms on my websites, feeding six different lists. And when I send out a broadcast email to all my lists at the same time, the platform automatically ensures nobody gets duplicate emails. Simple but powerful.

By the way, your intermediate content could also be a complimentary one-hour consultation or a property assessment or a portfolio analysis or website diagnostic or virtually anything. Take some time to think about your intermediate content. Start structuring it in a way where you can offer it to your prospects in return for information.

What are you really doing? You're qualifying your prospects, that's what! This is Sales 101. The people who request your intermediate content are demonstrating their interest in your expertise. They are demonstrating their trust in your knowledge. In Chapter 41, we'll give them something to *buy*!

Step-by-step action guide:

☐ *Decide what your intermediate content is.*
☐ *Make sure it's built and ready for delivery.*
☐ *Give it away for free to gather information.*
☐ *Select an email autoresponder provider.*
☐ *Create a sign-up form on their platform.*
☐ *Build a page on your website with the offer.*
☐ *Embed the sign-up form on your website.*
☐ *Sign up yourself to test the process.*
☐ *Describe your offer with a call-to-action.*
☐ *Include it with all your beginner content.*

Intermediate Content = List

41

Advanced Content = Revenue

Who's ready to make some money?!?

The past two chapters were about building a sales funnel with your beginner and intermediate content. We've been leaving bread crumbs on the path, letting people sample your expertise and pulling them through the sales funnel by enticing them with valuable carrots.

And in return for this value, you've captured some information about them. At the very least, you now know how to contact the ones who were truly interested in what you're offering. These are now warm prospects. They already know who you are.

The whole point is to qualify your prospects. At each stage, you're offering more value. Those who are no longer interested drop off but those who want more will stay with you. It's a sales funnel. You're providing value and building trust. Now, you have to sell them something!

Your advanced content can take a lot of different forms. Perhaps the final sales proposition is just a product and the beginner and intermediate content was only intended to show your knowledge of that product. Perhaps it's your services as a mortgage broker, financial advisor, insurance agent or real estate agent. Maybe it's a big information product or a membership program or an intensive three-day workshop.

Are you curious what mine is? My advanced content is my in-person speaking engagements. That's what I'm looking for. That's my passion. I speak about entrepreneurship, internet marketing and our changing economy. My message is one of empowerment and opportunity.

At this stage of my email course (tip #36), I ask my subscribers to consider me to speak at one of their events. Whether it be for a keynote address or a training workshop, my programs get rave reviews.

Tactical Execution > About > Speaking Engagements

My example serves two purposes. First, it pulls my audience further through *my* sales funnel. It tells my subscribers why I'm offering all this information. But second, it demonstrates my point for this chapter. Think about your own advanced content. What exactly are you selling? What problem are you solving? What *pain* are you alleviating?

Start a list of all the different things you could offer that fall into the advanced content category. Don't wait. You have to know where you're going. You have to know where you're leading your prospects.

In earlier chapters, we discussed building your website? Chapter 14 was all about knowing precisely what you want your website visitors to do. Why am I here? Remember? Most webmasters can't answer that simple question for their visitors. They don't have a clear idea of what they want their website visitors to do.

Not only do you need that clarity for the development of your website but you need it for your content categories and your revenue model as well. Define exactly what your advanced content is and how you plan to package it for your audience. For example, I don't recommend charging for your expertise by the hour. Instead, package a solution and charge a fee that reflects the value being delivered.

Refer back to Chapter 20 about "expanding the frame". It was about having a broader view of your business and offering different products at different price points to cater to the different objectives and passions of your audience. That all applies here too.

When structuring your advanced content solutions, be sure to include something very inexpensive – maybe just $10 – and other things that are very extravagant and expensive – maybe $4000 or more. Expand the frame. Broaden your perspective. Create a menu of products or services that spans far and wide!

Here's your opportunity to build a revenue model. Here's your opportunity to make some money. Don't let it slip through your fingers. You've earned it! You've demonstrated your expertise. You've provided value. You've built trust. Now, you have to start earning some money.

This is where it all comes together. We've covered a lot of structural elements. It's like building a house. You have to pour the concrete first. It takes time and rarely offers much visible progress from a distance. But once the foundation is built, the framers come in and the house goes up quickly.

We're at the framing stage. This is where you step out and ask your audience to buy something. This is often the hardest part because you have to believe in yourself first. That confidence should come from your growing list, but it takes time. It takes patience.

Always remember this: even if you still feel a bit shaky with your expertise, never underestimate the passion of your prospects. Never underestimate the confidence they already have in *you*. Never underestimate the need they have for your expertise.

Some of the people in your audience already *want* to take action. They *want* to move forward. They believe in you. They believe you can solve their problem. If you don't give them a way to take action, you are doing them a disservice.

Don't wait for 100% of your audience to be ready to buy. Some of them are ready now. Some of them are ready today. Give them what they want and worry about the others later.

Categorize your content. Package your value. And go make some money!

Step-by-step action guide:

- ☐ *Clarify your advanced content solutions.*
- ☐ *Determine price based on value delivered.*
- ☐ *Tell your audience about your solutions.*
- ☐ *Create a broad product or service menu.*
- ☐ *Offer both simple & extravagant solutions.*
- ☐ *Never underestimate your audience.*
- ☐ *Some of them are ready to take action.*
- ☐ *Cater to your most passionate prospects.*
- ☐ *Let your growing list build your confidence.*

Advanced Content = Revenue

42

Killer Sales Copy

Have you ever heard about the Motivating Sales Sequence?

I haven't used that phrase so far in this book, but we used the concept right at the beginning. We used it when we discussed your Elevator Pitch in Chapter 6.

The Motivating Sales Sequence is a basic sales process. It's a way of telling someone about something. With your Elevator Pitch, you were telling people about *you* but you can use the same process to tell them about your product or service.

This chapter is about using the Motivating Sales Sequence to write effective sales copy for your website. Effective sales copy equals higher conversion rates. That means a higher percentage of your website visitors actually *buy* something.

That's a good thing.

The Motivating Sales Sequence has seven specific steps. Each step gives the reader different information but they're all essential and the *order* of the steps is critically important as well!

Step #1: Get their attention.

Start with something amazing, shocking or provocative. Reference an incredible statistic. Make a controversial statement. Ask a provocative question. The opening sentences need to jolt your readers to attention.

Step #2: Identify the problem or need.

Once you have their attention, you need to identify the problem and the *pain* your product or service alleviates. People have lots of problems but they're only willing to spend money when the problem gives them some *pain*.

Step #3: Position your product as the solution.

Explain how your product solves the problem and alleviates the *pain*. Focus on the benefits, not the features. Better yet, describe the emotions – the emotions of the *pain* and the way your customers feel when the pain is gone.

Step #4: Differentiate yourself from the competition.

How are you different? What makes you better? This is where you present your Unique Selling Proposition (USP) and why your product or service is better than all the other options.

Step #5: Establish credibility and build value.

Explain why your product is worth more than the price. Describe your experience. Talk about your guarantees. Tell them how much *more* all the competitive products cost. Describe all the bonuses they get.

Step #6: Provide proof (statistics and testimonials).

Answer the instinctive question, "why should I believe you?" Here's where you pull out the statistics. Have you won any awards? Do you have any special credentials?

What about testimonials? Testimonials are extremely effective at building trust with your audience, especially if you include photos, audio or video.

Step #7: Close with a call-to-action.

This is the most important step. Ask for the sale. Be specific. Explain exactly what you want the reader to do. Missing this one step cuts your conversion in half. The people who are interested *want* to know how to take action. Don't deny them that opportunity.

And finally, give them something to *buy*!

Hopefully, by now, you understand what this process is designed to do. It's designed to walk people through a logical progression that offers *your* product as the best possible alternative. It's designed to position your product as the no-brainer solution to the painful problem your audience is struggling with.

Set some time aside to write sales copy for each of your products or services. You'll need an online description page for each of your products anyway. So do it. Do it now. Get it done. You'll be excited when you're done and you'll be one *big* step closer to making money online.

Step-by-step action guide:

☐ *Focus on each of your products individually.*
☐ *Take notes for each of the seven steps.*
☐ *Write each section of the sales sequence.*
☐ *Put it all together and work on the flow.*
☐ *Spend extra time on the call-to-action.*
☐ *Ask friends to read it and provide feedback.*

Killer Sales Copy

43

Making Sales Online

Are you selling your product or service online?

The last few chapters have discussed your expertise and how to categorize that information into beginner, intermediate and advanced content.

The advanced content is where you can finally make some money. Chapter 42 introduced the Motivating Sales Sequence to help you write sales copy for your advanced content products and services.

Your advanced content can take a lot of different forms. Maybe it's a product you sell. Maybe it's a professional service like providing insurance, originating loans or selling real estate. Maybe it's an information product that instructs buyers how to accomplish a specific objective.

Regardless what your advanced content is, you need to have a way of selling it online. You need a way to process the actual transactions.

Turns out, there are a ton of websites that host products and let you sell them using *their* shopping cart. These options make it incredibly easy to start making sales on the internet and we'll use this chapter to review a few of them.

Perhaps the best known online platform for making sales online is eBay. Most people know eBay as an auction site where you can make your products available for open bidding, but that's only the beginning.

http://www.ebay.com/

eBay allows its users to create their very own eBay store, featuring all of their products in one place. You can then put certain popular products into the public auction and use them to entice shoppers into your store. Also, eBay owns the widely-used PayPal platform, making it easy to send and receive money securely.

Its worthwhile noting that eBay is one of the highest traffic websites on the internet. It's crawling with literally millions of shoppers all the time. I call that a "raging river" and it's a great place to put your product in front of a massive buying audience quickly.

There are tons of resources devoted to leveraging the eBay opportunity and I recommend you simply put "selling products on eBay" into a Google search to get started.

eBay isn't the only place where you can create your own store. Yahoo offers a similar opportunity. The Yahoo Shopping network is a powerful and flexible platform that gives regular people an easy way to sell products on the internet.

http://shopping.yahoo.com/

Of course, one of the largest online retailers is Amazon. Well, as luck would have it, you can sell your products there too! Amazon has a number of seller programs including the Advantage program, making it easy to upload products and sell them to the public.

http://advantage.amazon.com/

Within the Advantage program, Amazon fulfils the orders for you. That means they ship your product to the customer. They also have a second seller platform where you fulfill the orders yourself. With eBay and Yahoo, the product delivery is always left to you.

With eBay and Yahoo, you're the retailer. With Amazon Advantage, you're the wholesaler and Amazon is the retailer. Because of that, the Advantage program takes a much larger cut. They get the first 55% of your product's sales price. But then, if you see a reduced price on Amazon, that discount comes out of *their* share, not yours.

Keep in mind that these programs are changing all the time. New websites are popping up every day and that increased competition improves these arrangements over time. Check to see what the latest programs offer and use the ones that suit your situation the best.

There are dozens of other places where you can sell your products, particularly if the product is digital (like an e-book or an audio file). Zipidee is a great example. On Zipidee, you can upload your digital products and sell them to the public.

http://www.zipidee.com/

The biggest advantage of these platforms is that they all have massive traffic already. That means you can put *your* product in front of *their* buyers, and not worry quite as much about generating your own traffic. Driving traffic is usually the hardest part!

Of course, you can also drive traffic to your own website or blog and then link through to these platforms. That means you can include a link on your sales page (with the killer sales copy you wrote in Chapter 42) that points to the website where your visitors can buy the product.

Step-by-step action guide:

☐ Visit eBay and read about their programs.
☐ Explore the Yahoo Shopping Network.
☐ Research the latest programs on Amazon.
☐ Check out Zipidee and look for others.
☐ Evaluate based on credibility and profits.
☐ Sell your products on the winning websites.
☐ Link to your products from your own site.

Making Sales Online

44

Website Shopping Cart

Do you want your very own shopping cart?

Chapter 43 looked at a variety of websites where you can sell your products online but we didn't look at selling stuff directly on your own website. That's what this chapter is about.

Having your own shopping cart is a lot easier than it used to be. There was a time when you had to build all the code into your own website. You had to integrate your website with a merchant account to accept VISA or MasterCard and you had to integrate that merchant account with your bank account.

It was complicated. No longer.

Today, there are companies that offer out-of-the-box shopping cart solutions that you can easily link to or integrate directly into your own website. In most cases, the people visiting your website don't even realize the shopping cart is being hosted elsewhere.

A great example is 1ShoppingCart.com.

The websites we discussed in the last chapter – eBay, Yahoo, Amazon and Zipidee – the ones that host your products and let you sell them using *their* shopping cart – make money on the product being sold. In other words, they get a cut of your sales price.

With 1ShoppingCart, you can sell whatever you want and get 100% of the money but they charge a fee for the shopping cart itself. They also operate as the merchant account so they make some money on the credit card transactions too.

There are advantages to both formats and we discussed some of the advantages of the first group in Chapter 43. In this chapter, we'll focus exclusively on 1ShoppingCart and the service they offer.

With 1ShoppingCart, you can sell anything for any price. It can be a $25 e-book, an $800 consulting solution, a $4,000 retreat package or a $17,000 custom motorcycle. It can also be a subscription or membership package, meaning your customers are automatically charged every month or every year or whatever you specify.

No matter what you're selling, 1ShoppingCart allows you to process online transactions in a flexible and seamless way. Even if you consummate an offline transaction without a computer nearby, you can take a credit card number and process the payment when you get back to the office.

1ShoppingCart has a variety of packages, each offering different levels of functionality. The most inexpensive packages start around $35 per month and their premium option is about $100, plus standard credit card processing fees.

The premium option includes an email autoresponder as well. The advantage is that everything exists on the same platform. At the time of this writing, I have my products on a variety of different platforms and my autoresponder with Aweber.

Although I'm very happy with Aweber, it can be frustrating to maintain content on so many different platforms. Also, if I make a sale on Amazon, I have no way of contacting the customer afterwards. They don't give me their email address. With 1ShoppingCart, I would have full contact information for all of my customers.

I've considered moving everything over to 1ShoppingCart, just to have it all together. Think about it. If you have everything on one platform, you can send different emails to different people depending on their individual history with you.

If they purchased one product, you can tailor an email acknowledging that. If they subscribed to your intermediate content but have not purchased anything yet, you can tailor an email to that as well. And for your best customers – the ones who have bought from you multiple times – you can send special offers that nobody else gets.

It's been proven time and again that marketing is more effective if it's more personalized. The less 'canned' your message sounds, the better. You want each reader to feel like you're speaking directly to him or her.

1ShoppingCart offers a powerful and flexible solution. The platform can calculate sales taxes and shipping rates automatically. It supports affiliate links and up-sell or cross-sell options. It offers secure SSL encryption for the checkout process and makes payment tracking simple. It's not the only solution but it's definitely one of the best.

If you're serious about selling stuff online, you'll need a shopping cart eventually. You can easily leverage other platforms but having your own comes with some distinct advantages. 1ShoppingCart is one option you should consider.

Step-by-step action guide:

- ☐ *Visit the <u>1ShoppingCart.com</u> website.*
- ☐ *Read about their various service options.*
- ☐ *Research other ecommerce platforms.*
- ☐ *Think about what you'd like to sell online.*
- ☐ *Make note of the features you could use.*
- ☐ *Consider subscribing to their service.*
- ☐ *Learn how to use the platform thoroughly.*
- ☐ *Leverage the service wherever possible.*

Website Shopping Cart

45

SEO: Keyword Saturation

Do people find you on Google?

The vast majority of websites get very few visitors through search engines. Why? Because your website might be on page 20 (or worse) for the keyword phrases you're targeting. Most people never get past page one or two of the search results.

Just look at a basic example. As of this writing, a search for the keyword phrase "internet marketing" brings up over 94 million results but Google's first page only has 10 listings. Assuming the searcher looks through two pages of results, 93,999,980 listings never even get seen.

Getting ranked high on search engines like Google has become a science. It's referred to as Search Engine Optimization (or SEO for short) and the next four chapters introduce some powerful tricks you can use to optimize your website for the search engines.

Let's start at the beginning. Search engines like Google look for three primary factors when determining website rankings.

1. The quantity of unique relevant content.
2. The newness or freshness of that content.
3. The link structure surrounding the website.

This chapter elaborates on the first factor. Chapter 46 introduces a great SEO trick and Chapter 47 elaborates on the third factor. The second speaks for itself. Don't let your website get stale. Continue to add more content and make adjustments to existing content. Keep it fresh. Google loves new content!

Let's jump into the first factor. Clearly, the basic message is that more is better. A 400-page website generally ranks higher than a four-page website. But there are a number of things you can do *within* the content to make it more search engine friendly.

First, Google loves sentences and paragraphs. Avoid bulleted lists and hidden text. Whenever possible, put your content into standard sentences and paragraphs.

Keywords, keywords, keywords. We talked about keyword research in Chapter 10 and 11 and here's where they belong! Pick about a dozen primary keyword phrases and use them naturally but consistently in the following places:

1. The primary domain name, if possible.
2. The page title and, ideally, the page URL.
3. Any H1 heading tags throughout your site.
4. The title tag and page description.
5. The alt tags of all images on your site.
6. The first paragraph of your page content.
7. Throughout your body text.

Let's drill down on a few of these. The first point is an often-missed opportunity. If you haven't already registered a domain name for your website, try to find one that incorporates your most important keyword. It helps.

The second point is also overlooked frequently. A lot of websites are structured such that the individual page URLs

end in things like ".com/content/pageid?=63956/".
Nothing could be less helpful from an SEO perspective.

The page URL is valuable real estate. Whenever possible, incorporate your page title into the page URL. Using your primary keywords in the page title and also in the page URL dramatically improves the odds of having that page rank high for the keywords used.

The third point is important as well. If you have any headings on your page, always use H1 tags and incorporate keywords into the heading. H1 is an HTML tag that refers to Heading #1. HTML also includes H2, H3 and H4 tags.

Google considers H1 tags to be important and weighs the words in H1 tags much higher than normal content. Take advantage of that by using H1 tags and incorporating your keywords in those titles.

The fourth point is missed entirely on most websites. Title tags and page descriptions cater directly to search engines but most websites don't even use them. That's a major missed opportunity. Not only will they have an immediate impact on your website's ranking but they also determine what shows up on the search engine results page.

The fifth point is an opportunity. Every image you put on your website can have an HTML alt tag. That determines the words that show up when someone uses their cursor to scroll over top of the image. Google looks at alt tags as an indication of what the image and the page are about so make sure you load them with keywords.

The sixth point seems trivial but it makes a difference. Google likes to see the primary keywords in the first paragraph. Also, make sure the keywords in your page title match the keywords being used in the page description and throughout the page content.

Once you've made adjustments to your website, you'll have to wait for Google to re-index your site before you'll see the results. That can take anywhere from a few hours to a few weeks depending on how often your site gets indexed.

You can resubmit your sitemap to accelerate the process. The Google Webmaster Tools is the easiest place to do that and we'll be introducing that platform in Chapter 48. You can also submit individual URLs manually at the following location.

http://www.google.com/addurl/

Done properly, the suggestions laid out in this chapter can dramatically improve your search engine ranking.

Step-by-step action guide:

- ☐ *Write in full sentences and paragraphs.*
- ☐ *Register a domain name with keywords.*
- ☐ *Include keywords in page titles & URLs.*
- ☐ *Use H1 tags and include your keywords.*
- ☐ *Always use title tags and page descriptions.*
- ☐ *Include keywords in all image alt tags.*
- ☐ *Use keywords in the first paragraph.*
- ☐ *Use keywords throughout body text.*

SEO: Keyword Saturation

46

SEO: Homepage Mentality

How many homepages does your website have?

The conventional wisdom is that your website has one homepage. Not necessarily true. You can have multiple homepages. You can design dozens of pages that *look* like homepages but are actually buried somewhere on your website and are precision-optimized for a particular keyword phrase.

My Tactical Execution website has 68 homepages. One is my actual homepage but there are 67 others that target various phrases. Depending on what you search for, Google lists the most appropriate one. When people click on the listing and land on my website, they almost never realize they're not on my actual homepage.

Not surprisingly, my primary homepage is:

http://www.tacticalexecution.com/

The other 67 homepages each target a different geographic location along with the phrase "internet marketing services." For example, I target San Francisco, Oakland, Berkeley and a variety of other municipalities in the Bay

Area, each with the same phrase. One such page can be found at the following URL:

> http://www.tacticalexecution.com/contact/san-
> francisco-internet-marketing-services/

As you can see, the page is called "San Francisco internet marketing services" and I have similar pages for "Oakland internet marketing services" and "Berkeley internet marketing services" and so on. These keyword phrases are also included in the page's URL as well as the title tag, page description, alt tags and body text.

These precision-optimized pages each rank nicely for the phrases they target. Think about it. If someone was searching for the phrase "Berkeley internet marketing services", my website offers an exact match, at least in terms of the page title and URL.

The thing to remember is that Google slices and dices internet content. It doesn't distinguish between your homepage and all the other pages on your website. If one particular page buried deep in your website is the best match for the keywords being searched for, that's the page that comes up.

The pages described above are precision-optimized for one particular keyword phrase and I have 67 of them, each targeting a slightly different phrase. The idea is to provide the search engines with a perfect destination page for someone searching for that particular keyword phrase.

This boils down to an understanding of how search engines work. People who find your website through a search engine may or may not land on your actual homepage first. For that reason, you should build your entire site as if each page had a homepage responsibility.

Build pages that cater to specific keyword phrases. If you know of a keyword phrase a lot of your prospects are searching for, build a page all about that phrase. Build an entire section about it! Give the search engines a reason to direct their users to your website.

Make sure these precision-optimized pages are well integrated into your website with plenty of links leading from other pages to these special targeted pages. Google looks at the internal link structure of a website almost as much as it looks at the external link structure.

An entire book could be written about optimizing the internal link structure on your website. It can make a huge difference. Cross-reference all the pages on your website with descriptive text links. It brings the information closer together and the search engines love that.

Step-by-step action guide:

- ☐ *Identify your top keyword phrases.*
- ☐ *Build one page all about each phrase.*
- ☐ *Include the phrase in the title and URL.*
- ☐ *Treat these pages as if they're homepages.*
- ☐ *Welcome visitors who see that page first.*
- ☐ *Build content that caters to search engines.*
- ☐ *Precision-optimize one phrase at a time.*
- ☐ *Maximize internal links to targeted pages.*

SEO: Homepage Mentality

47

SEO: Link Building Tricks

How many inbound links do you have?

Chapter 45 introduced the three primary factors the search engines look for when ranking different websites. Here they are again.

1. The quantity of unique relevant content.
2. The newness or freshness of that content.
3. The link structure surrounding the website.

The third factor is extremely important. Basically, Google considers an inbound link from a related content website to be a vote of confidence in your website. The more votes you have, the better your website is presumed to be.

Now, there are a lot of inbound links that don't mean much. Untargeted web directories that do not present related content are a good example. Link farms are another. As a result, Google gives you credit for some links but not others.

Google also looks at a second level to see how many links are pointing to the websites that are linking to you. So, if I had an inbound link from a website that had five inbound links itself, it would count for *less* than a different inbound link coming from a website that had 100 inbound links.

This methodology forms the foundation of the Google PageRank score. PageRank is a score Google calculates to reflect the relevance and importance of any particular website. The range is between 0 and 10 where 10 is the highest score. We talked about this in Chapter 35.

The Google PageRank score is calculated on a logarithmic curve so most websites have a score of three or lower. A PageRank of four is definitely above average. Predictably, Google has a PageRank of 10. Yahoo has a 9.

You can easily check your PageRank by installing the Google Toolbar or by using one of the many Google PageRank Checkers on the internet. You can also see the inbound links Google gives you credit for by entering:

| link:www.WebsiteName.com | **Search** |

Back to inbound links. A link from a PR7 (short for a website with a PageRank score of 7) is far more valuable than a link from a PR2. In fact, you could probably have 20 inbound links from PR2 websites and still rank lower than a competitor that has just one link from a PR7.

The number and quality of your inbound links determines your PageRank score. Once you start getting inbound links from PR5+ websites, your PageRank score goes up quickly. But for now, let's take a look at some inbound links you can easily create all by yourself.

Basically, we're looking for other related content websites to link to your website. There are a bunch of places where you can build a free website all by yourself and use it as a 'feeder' website to link to your primary 'hub' website. You also have full control over the content.

Right off the top of my head, I can think of a few places where you can build a feeder site to prop up your hub site.

1. WordPress.com
2. Blogger.com
3. Squidoo.com
4. Weebly.com
5. Webs.com
6. Sites by Google
7. Geocities by Yahoo
8. Angelfire by Lycos

In each case, you can build a little site for yourself without paying a penny. You can then load it with related content and include a bunch of links to the target pages on your primary hub website.

You can even optimize the links. You see, Google looks at the anchor text (the words carrying the link) as an indication of what the target website is about. If you put the link on the words "internet marketing services", the target website ranks higher for those words.

This is an incredibly powerful SEO strategy. Not only are you creating one-way inbound links to your primary website but you can put those links on the exact keywords you're trying to target.

Allocate some time to build four or five feeder websites using the platforms listed above. Load them all with related content and link them all to your primary website. Also, make sure they all link to each other, creating a virtual net for the search engine spiders.

Chapter 46 discussed the precision-optimized pages that act as alternative homepages for search engine users. You can improve the PageRank for those particular pages by linking directly to them (rather than your actual homepage) from your feeder sites.

Obviously, the problem is that these feeder sites are almost certainly low PageRank websites, at least at the beginning, so the inbound links won't mean much. But it's a start and you can continue to build up those feeder sites as time goes on. Add content from time to time and keep them fresh. The point is these are all things you control yourself. You don't have to ask anybody's permission.

There are many other strategies for building a robust link structure around your website and we'll be discussing many of them in the coming chapters. The reason for introducing this particular strategy here is because of its singular application as an SEO tactic.

Step-by-step action guide:

- ☐ *Identify your primary keyword phrases.*
- ☐ *Build 'feeder' sites on Web 2.0 platforms.*
- ☐ *Load feeder sites with related content.*
- ☐ *Add links to your primary 'hub' website.*
- ☐ *Put the links on your primary keywords.*
- ☐ *Point links to your primary target pages.*
- ☐ *Ensure all feeder sites link to each other.*
- ☐ *Keep the content on feeder sites fresh.*

SEO: Link Building Tricks

48

SEO: Diagnostic Tools

What SEO strategies have you missed? What mistakes have you made?

How could you know? After all, you *missed* them. How can you possibly know what tactics you forgot about? The good news is there are plenty of diagnostic tools on the internet that can help you identify problems or missed opportunities on your website.

This chapter introduces three of my personal favorites. None of them cost any money and they each offer tremendous insights to evaluate and improve your website.

Google Webmaster Tools
http://www.google.com/webmasters/tools/

Like so many other services, Google offers the webmaster tools platform free of charge. The platform has an impressive series of tools you can use to diagnose and fine-tune your website.

But before you can do anything, you need to verify that it is, in fact, your website. Don't worry. The verification is easy to do. Full instructions are provided.

Once verified, you can see any errors the Google spiders experienced when crawling your website. You can also see when Google visited your site and how many pages they crawled and/or indexed.

One important setting you can specify on the webmaster tools platform is your preferred domain format. In case you didn't know, the "www" at the beginning of most domain names is actually optional. You don't *need* to include it. But there's a problem.

Let's assume your website *has* the "www" in the complete URL. People who link to your website *without* the "www" experience an automatic redirect. In other words, they *will* get to your website but only because the computer knows to redirect them.

Those redirected links work but they're not precise. Because they're not direct, they don't count as an inbound link from a search engine perspective. Unless ...

Google Webmaster Tools allows you to specify your preferred domain format, either *with* or *without* the "www". It's under the Settings tab and I recommend you do that immediately. It ensures that links using either format count as legitimate inbound links.

The platform also allows you to view a series of diagnostic summaries, index statistics, internal/external links and your sitemap. You can even analyze and/or generate a robot.txt file to help Google navigate your website.

Google Webmaster Tools is a powerful platform. Take advantage of it.

The SEO-Browser
http://www.seo-browser.com/

SEO Browser is a brilliant tool that shows you what your website looks like to a search engine. If you visit the site, I recommend you click on the "Advanced" tab in the top right-hand corner and then enter your domain name in the search field.

The tool shows you exactly what a search engine sees … and what it does *not* see. In other words, it shows you the opportunities you're missing. It shows you places where you can enter more descriptive keywords and headings.

The nice thing about the SEO Browser is that you can navigate around your site by clicking on the various links and it stays inside the tool and shows you the search engine perspective throughout. Try it. Browse your site.

It also tells you how many internal and external links are on each page. The Google webmaster guidelines recommend you limit the outbound links on any particular page to 100. The SEO Browser tells you immediately if you have exceeded that number.

Chapter 45 discussed Google's preference for sentences and paragraphs. Bottom line; Google loves lots of content. The SEO Browser calculates the "text to page weight ratio", offering valuable insight to how search engines evaluate the density of written content on your website.

Another important measure is the size of the page in terms of memory and how quickly it loads. You want your webpages to require as little memory as possible, allowing for quicker load times. Poorly optimized images are the most common culprit for slow-loading pages.

The SEO Browser provides dozens of valuable insights. Check it out.

Website Grader
http://website.grader.com/

Website Grader takes a much broader view of your website and attempts to assess its marketing effectiveness compared with other websites on the internet. It looks at things like page optimization, load times, syndication options, domain registration and social media presence.

The tool isn't that great from a strictly SEO perspective but it does a fantastic job of reminding you about all the different angles of an effective website. Run the tool on your website and see what it suggests. I guarantee it will put a few items on your to-do list.

By the way, the Website Grader gives you a score out of 100, telling you how your site ranked compared with all the other sites it looks at. I recommend you ignore it. Most websites are a complete disaster so a good score from this tool does *not* mean you have a great website. It just means you did better than some others.

Keep in mind that the top 1% of websites account for the vast majority of all online transactions. That means you should be shooting for a score of 99 or higher. Don't get too excited about a 70 or 80. We still have work to do!

Step-by-step action guide:

☐ *Visit the Google Webmaster Tools website.*
☐ *Create an account and verify your website.*
☐ *Select your preferred domain format.*
☐ *Check for broken links and other errors.*
☐ *Visit the SEO Browser and click Advanced.*
☐ *Enter your URL and browse your website.*
☐ *Look for opportunities to add keywords.*
☐ *Ensure each page has less than 100 links.*
☐ *Monitor the "text to page weight ratio."*
☐ *Visit the Website Grader and run your site.*
☐ *Review their suggestions for improvement.*

SEO: Diagnostic Tools

49

Build Massive Credibility

Why should I listen to YOU?!?

Credibility sits at the heart of business success, particularly if you're a service professional or a subject matter expert where people rely on your expertise. Luckily, modern technology has created tons of great opportunities to demonstrate expertise and build credibility fast.

The rest of this book discusses different strategies to demonstrate your expertise online and drive traffic to your website. But first, we'll use this chapter to focus on two amazing opportunities that will build more credibility than any of the others.

Record your own CD

The first is to record and produce an informational CD product – or a series of informational CD products. It's easier than you might think and the production costs are shockingly low.

Keep in mind that you can download the open source (that means free) Audacity recording software, buy a decent microphone with a pop filter and you're ready to go. Refer back to Chapter 21 for more details about effective audio recording techniques.

A typical CD runs about 70 minutes. Personally, I speak at a rate of about 140 words per minute. That means a CD represents about 10,000 words. In a standard Word document, that's about 20 pages of content. If you have an outline, you could probably write it out over a weekend.

Here's another approach. You can have a friend do an interview with you and record the whole thing. You could write a bunch of questions and prepare all your answers ahead of time. If you take this approach, you'll need a second microphone and a jack splitter to plug into your laptop.

As of this writing, I have 11 CDs available for sale on Amazon. To produce them, I use Kunaki.com in New York State. Their customer service is pretty weak but you can't beat the prices. The CDs cost just $1.75 each (including the jewel case, UPC barcode, cellophane wrapping and full color printing) and they have absolutely *no* minimums.

Did you catch that?? No minimums! That means you can order one CD and it will cost you less than $2.

Kunaki also makes it easy to sell your CDs on Amazon and other online retail platforms. When I get reorder Purchase Orders from Amazon, I place the order with Kunaki and they ship directly to the Amazon distribution center in Lexington, Kentucky.

Write a book. Become an author.

The second opportunity is to write a book. Wow. Did I just say that? Isn't that a huge task?? Yes, it is. But it's not as daunting as you might think. And as with CDs, there are places where you can get your book professionally printed with absolutely no minimums.

Let's start with the actual writing part. I've gone through this twice and feel totally differently about the project than I did before I started. It's not as hard as I thought but you have to be smart about it.

The most important step is to write a detailed outline. If you spent an hour or two each day, this step would still take at least a week to complete. Break it down. Organize your thoughts. Put bullet points under each chapter with the topics you want to cover. Move things around until you're happy with it.

Although there is no standard format, you probably want to plan for at least 10 or 12 chapters. Make sure you have five or six bullet points (or more) under each one. The idea is to have a series of specific topics where you can write about two or three pages on each one.

Let's break down the numbers briefly. In a typical Word document, one page contains about 500 words. But in a trade 6 x 9" book format, one page only contains about 300 words. So three book pages is about 900 words which equals about two pages in a Word document.

Let's assume you have 12 chapters with eight bullet points under each. That's a total of 96 bullet points. Let's further assume you wrote two bullet points in each sitting and you wrote two pages in a Word document for each bullet point. That's four pages in a Word document (about 2000 words) and about six pages in book format.

Personally, if I'm writing from a detailed outline, I can usually write about 1000 words per hour so 2000 words would take me two hours, and that's about my limit before my brain turns to butter. Anyway, that means I could finish two bullet points in one sitting. It also means I could finish all 96 bullet point in 48 sittings.

If I did one each working day (Monday to Friday), it would take me 10 weeks to complete. Add the outline at the beginning and I'm looking at 11 weeks total. That's less than three months!

Admittedly, after writing the book, there's still a huge job editing and publishing but all that stuff is easier to do when the content is already complete.

Although there are many print-on-demand (POD) suppliers, I use Lulu.com and am thrilled with their service and capabilities. My first book *"Make Yourself Useful, Marketing in the 21st Century"* has a total of 236 pages and it sells on Amazon for $23.95. To print just one copy – just *one* copy – costs $9.17 plus shipping. That's a bargain!

Nothing builds credibility like writing a book. Nothing. You only become an author once. After you've completed your first book, you remain an author for the rest of your life. It's a big deal. Consider undertaking the project. Become an author … for the rest of your life!

Kunaki and Lulu are amazing resources. They both allow you to build impressive credibility pieces with no minimums. That's an amazing opportunity and one that can change your career forever.

Step-by-step action guide:

- ☐ Visit *Kunaki.com* and see their capabilities.
- ☐ Search for other CD production providers.
- ☐ Think about creating your own CD product.
- ☐ Visit *Lulu.com* and read about their service.
- ☐ Search for other print-on-demand options.
- ☐ Consider writing your very own book.
- ☐ Commit to writing a detailed book outline.
- ☐ Try to allocate the time to get it done.

Build Massive Credibility

50

Understand the Process

How do you drive traffic to a website?

The rest of this book (this chapter and the next nine) is devoted to answering that question. There are tons of different strategies but we'll be focusing on the most powerful organic strategies being used today.

Before we get started, we have to introduce the internet marketing process in general. And in its most basic form, it's a very simple process.

Understanding the Internet Marketing Process		
Get people to your website ...	*... and impress them once they get there.*	
Drive Traffic.	**Provide Value.**	**Monetize Trust.**

Get people to your website ... and impress them once they get there. Simple. Two basic steps. A good portion of this book has dealt with the second step and it's worth noting that it can be broken down into two parts. Build trust first and then monetize that trust second.

Nobody is going to buy anything from you unless they trust you first. I've repeated this throughout this book and it's critically important. But without website traffic, even *that* doesn't matter!

The next nine chapters deal with the first step: driving traffic. Let's look at the process from a conceptual perspective. Essentially, the idea is to populate the internet with valuable demonstrations of your expertise along with links back to your website. We want to show people how great you are and then give them a way to learn more.

You live in a home. Your home has one front door. That's not the case for your website. Your website can have hundreds or even thousands of front doors. Any place that has a link to your website represents another front door. It's one more way to enter your website.

The idea behind driving traffic to your website is to put an attractive front door right in the middle of a huge crowd of your ideal customers. Figure out where they're browsing the internet and then demonstrate your expertise right in front of them, along with a link to your website.

This process contributes to your SEO objectives as well because it adds more inbound links to your website, increasing your Google PageRank score.

You can think about it like fishing. You want to throw some tasty bait into a raging river. The raging river is a website with tons of traffic. The tasty bait is your demonstration of expertise.

You need both. If you put great bait in a small stream, you won't get anything. If you throw rotten bait into a raging river, you'll get nothing. But if you find a combination of great bait and raging rivers, you'll hit the jackpot and you can repeat the same process over and over again.

This process implies two parts. First, you have to find raging rivers full of your ideal customers. There's no sense promoting a senior's living facility on MySpace. It's the wrong audience. MySpace would be a better place to promote dating sites, music bands or video games.

Second, you have to refine your bait to make it as appetizing and enticing as possible. Once you've found your target market, you have to demonstrate your expertise such that your audience wants to learn more.

The next nine chapters introduce some powerful strategies but the process is the same for almost any campaign. Even pay-per-click or banner advertisements follow the same basic model by promoting your value on a busy website and providing a link. It's all the same.

Step-by-step action guide:

☐ *Find your ideal customers on the internet.*
☐ *Identify raging rivers where they browse.*
☐ *Demonstrate your expertise on those sites.*
☐ *Give them a link to learn more about you.*
☐ *Repeat the process over and over again.*

Understand the Process

51

Publish Articles Online

Would you like your articles to be published on a high traffic website?

Of course you would. The first powerful strategy we'll cover is article marketing. Not only does it drive targeted traffic to your website but it also builds credibility and positions you as an expert in your field.

Here's the process. Write an article demonstrating your expertise. It doesn't have to be long; just 500 to 700 words. Once complete, there are tons of article directories where you can publish your article along with an 'Author Resource Box' where you can plug your website and include a link.

iSnare.com is an article directory that also has an article distribution service. For less than $2, you can distribute your article to thousands of different websites.

http://www.isnare.com/

It makes sense to understand the revenue model of these article directories. They want as many articles as they can get and they line the sides of their website with advertisements and hope their readers click on the ads. If they do, the article directory gets a small commission.

The moral of the story is that they don't really care if your article is good or not. They just want the content. In other words, you don't have to be a recognized expert to get 'published' on these directories. You could be anyone.

In 2007, I ran an experiment and published 70 articles in 70 days. By the end, a Google search for "Patrick Schwerdtfeger" (I have a pretty unusual last name!) brought up over 90,000 results. That means my articles had been published in 90,000 different places, each with a link back to my website.

My website had over 90,000 front doors!

Imagine the credibility I get when someone Googles my name and sees thousands of results, each referencing me as the expert author of one article or another.

The other nice thing about article marketing is that the articles stay out there for a long time, generating traffic to my website month after month. Over a year after my test, I was still getting traffic from all those articles I wrote.

By the way, I said earlier that the distribution service costs less than $2. The truth is that it costs one 'credit'. If you only buy a few credits, they cost about $1.80 each but if you buy a whole bunch, they cost less than $1. Knowing I was going to publish a lot of articles, I bought a lot of credits so the whole exercise cost me less than $70.

One article directory dominates the category. It's called EzineArticles.com and over 80% of my article marketing traffic came from that one website.

> http://www.ezinearticles.com/

If you plan to use this strategy to build credibility and drive traffic to your website, be sure to include EzineArticles.com in your campaign. Not only is it a great platform but it also provides unparalleled visibility to your readership and click-thru statistics.

Article marketing provides another terrific opportunity and it relates to the link you can include in the Author Resource Box at the bottom of each article. As mentioned in Chapter 47, the words that carry the link to your website are included in the search engine algorithms.

It's called "anchor text" and it is viewed as a good indication of the value offered by the destination website. If website A links to website B and the link sits on the words "internet marketing", the search engines assume that website B is a good place for people to learn about internet marketing.

When publishing articles, you can write your own Author Resource Box and put the link on any words you choose. That represents a great opportunity to boost your website's ranking for your primary keyword phrase.

Article marketing is a great way to populate the internet with your expertise, establish some credibility, drive some traffic to your site and improve your search engine ranking, all at one time.

Step-by-step action guide:

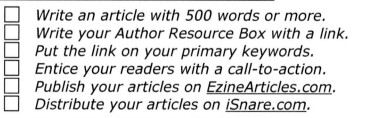

- ☐ *Write an article with 500 words or more.*
- ☐ *Write your Author Resource Box with a link.*
- ☐ *Put the link on your primary keywords.*
- ☐ *Entice your readers with a call-to-action.*
- ☐ *Publish your articles on EzineArticles.com.*
- ☐ *Distribute your articles on iSnare.com.*

Publish Articles Online

52

Post on Blogs & Forums

What's the most immediate traffic-generating strategy?

I've tested a lot of different things and the most immediate strategy by far is posting on popular internet forums. So what's a forum? Let's start with a definition.

Forums are essentially places where online conversations take place. Each individual conversation is called a 'thread'. Here's how it works. Members of the forum can start a thread by asking a question or making a statement. Then other members can enter the thread and provide an answer or contribute their thoughts about the original statement.

Soon, the thread grows to include contributions from multiple members, each demonstrating their expertise. You see, they're all using the forum to drive traffic to their own websites, just like you and me. And because they all want to impress each other with their knowledge and insights, forums are among the best places to learn about your field.

When you become a member of a forum, you can create a profile for yourself including links to your website. In some cases, you can even create a signature similar to an email signature. Every time you contribute to a thread and demonstrate your expertise, your signature appears immediately below your comments. That signature can include a link to your website.

The idea is to contribute some useful information or insights to the conversation, enticing other members to click through to your own website. Remember, every link is another 'front door' to enter your website and learn more about you.

Popular forums often have thousands of active threads going at one time. Every time someone adds a comment to a particular thread, it moves to the very top of the list. Then, when someone adds a comment to a different thread, the first thread moves down one notch and the second thread takes its place at the top of the list.

Obviously, the threads at the top of the list get the most traffic. I call that the 'fast water' and you want your contributions to be in the fast water as much as possible. Contributing to the most active threads is a good strategy. Not only will your contribution push it to the top of the list, but other people's contributions will keep it up there after you're gone.

As I said at the beginning, this strategy has the most immediate impact on your website's traffic. You can literally create an account on a popular forum, post some comments on active threads and see referral traffic on your website within a single hour.

How can you find popular forums in your field? There are two easy ways. First, visit Big-Boards and do a search for your keywords. It lists the biggest forums in your area.

http://directory.big-boards.com/

Second, do a search in Google for your keywords plus the word "forum". You can rest assured that whatever comes up at the top is a high-traffic forum.

Most online forums keep track of the number of contributions you've made and that statistic becomes a measure of your credibility and activity level within the community. As a result, your contributions won't get as much attention when you only have a few posts as they will when you have a lot of posts.

Once you've accumulated a reasonable number of posts (over 100 for example), try starting your own thread. It makes sense that the top comments within a thread are seen the most. If you initiate the thread yourself, your comments are at the top of that thread.

Ask an interesting question. Offer a list of resources. Make a provocative statement. You want your thread to become active. You want other forum members to see your thread and *want* to contribute. If you succeed, you'll be in the fast water for a longer time period and that will drive more traffic to your website.

There are a lot of people who sustain their entire business on forums. I spend a lot of time on the Warrior Forum (the largest forum about internet marketing) and some members have over 8,000 posts. Their comments are worth gold and they build impressive fan bases as a result.

Blogs are another great place to post comments. In fact, the ability for readers to post comments is one of the primary characteristics of blogs. Again, you can include a link along with your comment. The trick is to find the blog posts that rank high for your keywords and then make your contributions there.

One great place to search for popular blogs is Technorati.

http://www.technorati.com/

Another is Google BlogSearch.

http://blogsearch.google.com/

Visit them both. Search for your keywords. Find popular blog posts that rank high on the search engines. Read those posts and contribute your own thoughts to the conversation. If your comments provide real value, other readers will click on your link to learn more about you.

Blogs and forums are at the heart of today's social internet. Be part of the conversation. Demonstrate your expertise. Provide value. The rest takes care of itself.

Step-by-step action guide:

- ☐ *Search Big-Boards.com for your keywords.*
- ☐ *Use Google to find big forums in your field.*
- ☐ *Get an account and build your profile.*
- ☐ *Read a few threads before writing anything.*
- ☐ *Select threads where you can contribute.*
- ☐ *Provide value to the conversation.*
- ☐ *Never over-promote your own website.*
- ☐ *Start your own value-based threads.*
- ☐ *Search for popular blogs in your field.*
- ☐ *Post comments with a link to your website.*
- ☐ *Demonstrate your expertise, provide value.*

Post on Blogs & Forums

53

Post on Yahoo & Amazon

How can you leverage Yahoo and Amazon?

Turns out, there are easy ways to do both. Let's start with Yahoo.

Chapter 52 talked about posting comments on popular blogs and forums. The idea was to demonstrate your expertise right in front of a huge crowd of your ideal customers, enticing them to visit your website.

One of the largest forums on the internet is Yahoo Answers. Users either ask questions or provide answers. You can find just about every question you can imagine on Yahoo Answers. In fact, if you're ever curious about something, check there first. In most cases, you'll get the answers you need.

The interesting thing about Yahoo Answers is that users can rate the answers provided by others. The answer with the most votes is labeled as the best answer and the person who provided it is given credit. In fact, every answer is accompanied by a note stating how many 'best answers' that person has provided.

This feature lends incredible credibility to those who provide good information. After all, these answers are all being evaluated by your peer group. This transparency creates a tremendous opportunity for those who contribute real value to their community.

The way the platform is structured allows people with true expertise to rise to the top and get acknowledged for the value they provide. If you have true expertise, you can benefit from that process.

Yahoo Answers is a huge platform with massive traffic. The people who are well established on Yahoo Answers have a steady stream of ideal customers knocking at their door.

Think about it. Who would find your answers? The only people who would find your contributions are those who are searching for the questions you provided answers to. The only people who would find you are precisely those who need your expertise.

That's the most fascinating thing about the internet. Unlike the offline world, you can target your ideal customer with incredible precision. By selecting the questions you have answers to, you are automatically demonstrating your expertise *only* to those who need your knowledge.

Let's talk about Amazon. Most people know Amazon as an online book seller but they actually sell much more than that. But let's focus on books.

When you look for books on Amazon, you can read the reviews of others who have read them before you. Many people rely on those reviews more than the regular product description. Well, you can write those reviews just like anyone else.

Once again, the process allows for precision targeting. Who will find you? The only people who will find you are those who are considering the book you have already read; the people who want the knowledge you already have. By writing reviews for your favorite how-to books, you are demonstrating your expertise to your ideal customers.

Like Yahoo Answers, Amazon has a ton of traffic – millions of unique visitors each month. Writing reviews is a great way to demonstrate your expertise in the middle of a raging river, full of prospects you can target with precision.

On both platforms, Yahoo and Amazon, there are ways to point people to your website. On Yahoo Answers, you can put a link to your website in your profile description.

It's a little harder on Amazon. They have removed the ability to add live links in your profile but you can include your URL in your profile name. That puts your website address right beside every review you write.

Some of these strategies are a better match than others. Select the ones that work well with your business model and your expertise. Within each strategy, there are people who sustain their entire business by mastering that particular technique. You can do it too.

Step-by-step action guide:

- [ ] *Visit Yahoo Answers and get an account.*
- [ ] *Search for questions using your keywords.*
- [ ] *Read the questions people have asked.*
- [ ] *Read the answers people have contributed.*
- [ ] *Contribute your own expertise if possible.*
- [ ] *Don't post unless your answer is strong.*
- [ ] *Find your favorite books on Amazon.*
- [ ] *Read the reviews others have contributed.*
- [ ] *Create an account and include your URL.*
- [ ] *Write reviews for the best selling books.*

Post on Yahoo & Amazon

54

Upload Videos to YouTube

Are videos too complicated for you?

You might think so. You might also think YouTube only has trashy videos of people falling off their bikes or celebrities getting out of fancy sports cars. In both cases, you're wrong.

First, despite what you might think, the opportunity on YouTube is just getting started. And it's the misperceptions that prove the point. Indeed, the early adopters of YouTube used it for trashy pop-culture videos but the fastest growing segment right now is educational content.

I mentioned YouTube in the second chapter of this book. I suggested you visit YouTube and do a search for your keywords. If you did, you probably noticed that there are tons of educational videos your competitors are making to demonstrate their expertise to potential customers.

There is a *huge* opportunity to create educational video content on YouTube.

Second, creating videos is a lot easier than you might think. The process is made even easier by the trend towards authenticity in modern marketing. If the video is too slick, people don't trust it. They think it was created by a marketing agency and offers nothing more than another deceptive corporate marketing message.

Alternatively, if the video is more basic and amateur looking, people see it as authentic and more trustworthy. What a spectacular development! That means you can make basic educational videos and actually benefit from the less-than-perfect production quality.

If the *content* is good, the video will find an audience.

The latest product catering precisely to this market is the Flip video recorder. You can buy it for about $110 and record simple videos at the touch of a button. Better yet, the software required to use it is preinstalled on the device. All you have to do is plug it into your USB port and it helps you crop your video, make basic adjustments and upload directly to YouTube.

My point is that it isn't as complicated as you might think. Most people are intimidated by video and think it's beyond their reach. Not so.

The other thing to remember is that video is the richest form of media. Text is first, audio is second and video is at the top. For the viewer, it's the easiest and richest way to receive information. Not only do you get the underlying information but you also get to hear the voice of the creator and you might even see what he or she looks like.

One of the reasons YouTube has done so well is because they make it very easy to embed videos onto your own website. Once you upload a video file to YouTube, they give you a piece of code that allows you to display it on your website and the content streams directly from the YouTube servers. That means your server doesn't have to carry the heavy load of streaming video.

Video is the future. If you want to position yourself for tomorrow's internet users, start making videos.

Let's get into the logistics. For the purposes of educational YouTube videos, there are basically two types of recording. First, you can record a live situation with you talking about the topic. Second, you can record a screen capture from your computer.

By screen capture, I'm referring to those videos where it looks like you're watching someone's computer screen. You don't see the person. You only see their computer screen and hear their voice, narrating the presentation.

They might be demonstrating how to use a piece of software or a website and you can watch them move their mouse around and explain their activities. Or you might be watching a PowerPoint presentation with audio narration, all captured as a video.

This format of screen capture videos is even easier than trying to record yourself speaking about a topic. With a screen capture, you don't even have to worry about how you look! The viewer never sees you. They only see what's on your screen, accompanied by your voice.

There are a variety of software options to record screen capture videos. Some cost money and others are free. I recommend searching for "screen capture video recording software" and reviewing the listings that come up.

Here are two quick points in closing. First, always include your website address on your video – at the beginning, at the end and during the whole thing if possible. Remember, this exercise is designed to do two things: build credibility and drive traffic to your website.

Second, YouTube has a 10-minute limit for non-partners (you need thousands of viewers to become a partner). But that's okay because most people don't want to watch more than four or five minute videos anyway. So don't make one huge video. Instead, make a series of small videos and brand them all similarly so they 'belong' together.

After each video, YouTube automatically recommends related videos. If your series is all branded consistently, the related videos will direct viewers to others in the series. That way, each individual video can attract viewers who will then find the rest of your collection.

YouTube offers a tremendous opportunity to those willing to engage the technology and build content. I hope you give it a try.

Step-by-step action guide:

- ☐ *Search for your keywords on YouTube.*
- ☐ *Watch the educational videos that come up.*
- ☐ *Search for the Flip recorder on Amazon.*
- ☐ *Research other camcorder options.*
- ☐ *Brainstorm topics you could cover on video.*
- ☐ *Buy the necessary equipment.*
- ☐ *Select in-person or screen capture format.*
- ☐ *Try recording your first YouTube video.*
- ☐ *Get an account (a "channel") and upload.*
- ☐ *Tell all your friends where they can find it.*

Upload Videos to YouTube

55

Online Classified Advertising

What's the ugliest website on the internet? Craigslist!!

Craigslist is one of the most basic websites imaginable. It's nothing more than a huge bulletin board. No graphics. No fancy colors. Just text links and hundreds of thousands of advertisements. But as of this writing, it's the 12th most popular website in the country (according to Alexa).

Craigslist is a raging river. The website boasts over 50 million visitors self-publishing over 30 million classified ads every month. Is there a way to leverage that traffic and gain some exposure? Absolutely. Let's take a look.

As you probably know, Craigslist posts the most recent ad at the top and all the other ads in reverse chronological order down the page. When you first post your ad, it's at the very top. But as soon as someone else posts a different ad, your ad drops down to second place. When a third person posts an ad, yours drops down to third place, and so on.

Obviously, the ads at the top get most of the traffic. That's the fast water. When your ad drops down 100 spots or more, you're on the second page and your exposure drops off dramatically. If you want to stay in the fast water, you need to post new ads as often as possible.

The interesting thing about Craigslist is that they don't allow you to post the same ad on consecutive days. In fact, they have a seven day rotation. That means you can run the same ad every Monday or every Tuesday but not more often than that. Turns out, that's good news.

If you want to post new ads on Craigslist once each day, you need to write different versions in order to avoid the duplicate ad restrictions. Well, the process of writing different versions of your ad actually forces you to test different wording.

Testing is at the heart of internet success. You have to test to see what generates good results and what does not. Craigslist forces you to test your ad copy and that helps you improve your message. "Discover" tests higher than "learn". "Free" tests higher than "cheap". It won't take long and you'll start seeing what works and what doesn't.

You should also test the location of your ads. There are dozens of different categories on Craigslist and they each attract different users searching for different things. Some categories get very little traffic while others get tons.

For example, the 'women looking for men' personals ads get tons of visitors. The employment ads get tons of visitors. Apartments for rent ads get tons of visitors. Cars for sale get tons of visitors.

Meanwhile, other categories get far less traffic. 'Services' is a good example. This category is designed for people who want to advertise their professional services – plumbers, real estate agents, lawyers and insurance agents. Not surprisingly, there are tons of listings but not many visitors.

Get creative with your ad placement. Done properly, you should be able to post your message in at least two or three places. Again, you'll need different versions to do so but you'll also touch different audiences in the process.

A past client does large scale commercial lending. He only does loans larger than $10 million. He makes great money and his *only* advertising is on Craigslist. He posts two ads every morning, Monday to Friday, and gets between five and 10 inquiries per day.

Not only has he tested different ad copy and different category placement but he has also tested different cities. Craigslist has over 500 city platforms in over 50 different countries. Here in America, they have every major city covered. Because he can lend anywhere across the country, he tested different cities to see where he got the best results. Today, he only posts his ads in southern states like Oklahoma, Arkansas and Louisiana.

Another client does Feng Shui home assessments and she posted ads in the Gigs section of Craigslist. Because the Gigs section is similar to the employment listings, it gets a lot of traffic. The ad asked homeowners to fill out a detailed survey about interior décor. Participants were paid $5 and all of the completed surveys were entered into a raffle for a complimentary Feng Shui consultation.

Her ad got a good response and she promptly called each participant to inform them that *they* were the winner. Everyone won! After all, that's what she was looking for in the first place. Everyone won an in-person Feng Shui assessment in their own home.

It gave her a perfect opportunity to demonstrate her expertise to her ideal customers and potentially get hired to adjust their interior décor along Feng Shui principals. She used Craigslist to build a list of highly targeted prospects for her service.

Get creative! Craigslist is a raging river. Allocate some time to write five different versions of an ad promoting your product or service. Run one each day and use Google

Analytics to see which yields the *worst* response. Improve the worst one and run them again next week.

Each week, improve the ad yielding the worst response. Doing so ensures you remain on a continuous improvement trajectory. Over time, your ads will get better and better, and you'll be well on your way to an effective Craigslist advertising campaign.

Step-by-step action guide:

- ☐ *Search Craigslist for your keywords.*
- ☐ *Read the ads your competitors are posting.*
- ☐ *Notice which sections they are posting in.*
- ☐ *Write an advertisement for your business.*
- ☐ *Get creative with your approach and offer.*
- ☐ *Include either a link or accept emails.*
- ☐ *If using a link, use analytics to measure.*
- ☐ *Post your ad and measure the results.*
- ☐ *Write different versions of your ad.*
- ☐ *Test each ad to see which is most effective.*
- ☐ *Always improve the worst performing ad.*
- ☐ *Run ads regularly and monitor results.*

Online Classified Advertising

56

Pay-Per-Click Advertising

Would you spend 50¢ to speak with a qualified prospect?

You'd be crazy not to. That's the cheapest sales strategy available! So what if you could pay the same price to bring someone to your website? Is that a good deal? If you've followed the advice in this book and built a website that speaks to its visitors and leads them down a path to provide value and build trust, it might just work.

Pay-per-click (PPC) advertising allows you to display an advertisement to people who use a search engine to search for specific keywords that you select. If you sell Persian carpets, you can select those words and have your ad show up for precisely those people who are searching for Persian carpets. Once again, unlike the offline world, you can target your audience with unparalleled accuracy.

The other cool thing about PPC advertising is that you only get charged if someone clicks on your ad and lands on your website. If they don't click, it doesn't cost a penny.

The Google PPC program is called Google Adwords. Yahoo and MSN offer similar programs but this chapter focuses on the Google Adwords program.

http://adwords.google.com/

Does every click cost 50¢? No. Some cost more and others cost less. This chapter explains the basics of the system and how it works.

The cost to have your ad show up for a particular keyword phrase depends on how many other people are competing for the same keyword phrase. It operates similar to an auction. If the demand for that phrase is high, it costs more. If the demand is low, it costs less.

Here's the interesting thing. If you know what you're doing, you can find better qualified prospects for *less* money. Let me explain.

Someone searching for the word "carpet" on Google is probably *not* a buyer. They don't know exactly what they're looking for. If they did, they would've used more words in their query. Searching for just one word is far too broad. They're probably just kicking tires.

Consider someone who searches for "antique silk Persian carpet". Now, *that* person is a buyer! And they proved it by entering four words into their Google search. They know *exactly* what they want and they're probably ready to buy.

Which keyword phrase do you think has more competition: "carpet" or "antique silk Persian carpet"? You guessed it! The first phrase has more competition and costs far more than the second phrase. Meanwhile, the prospect searching for the first phrase is just kicking tires while the prospect searching for the second phrase is ready to buy.

Most people who do PPC advertising pay far too much for their clicks because they're using short generic keyword phrases. If the person who sells Persian carpets selected that one keyword phrase, it would cost far more than if he or she selected a variety of longer more descriptive phrases. Consider the following:

1. antique silk Persian carpet
2. antique wool Persian carpet
3. vintage silk Persian carpet
4. vintage wool Persian carpet
5. refurbished silk Persian carpet
6. refurbished wool Persian carpet
7. antique silk Persian rug
8. antique wool Persian rug
9. vintage silk Persian rug
10. vintage wool Persian rug
11. refurbished silk Persian rug
12. refurbished wool Persian rug

By selecting 12 descriptive keyword phrases that have four words each, the cost per click would be much lower and the ads would only display for higher quality prospects. Back in 2004, Chris Anderson described this as the long tail. By targeting long tail phrases, you'll attract better quality prospects for less money.

A properly optimized Google Adwords campaign might target hundreds or even thousands of long tail keyword phrases. Start writing down some of the phrases you might like to target.

There's one more thing that helps determine how much you pay for a particular keyword phrase and that's your Quality Score. The Quality Score looks at the keywords you're targeting, the keywords in the actual ad and the keywords on the landing page. If the keywords are consistent throughout, you get a high Quality Score. If not, you get a low Quality Score.

Obviously, Google doesn't want its Adwords clients to target high-traffic keywords to try and sell them something completely unrelated. That would frustrate users. So Google developed the Quality Score to ensure ads on the Google platform are relevant for users.

Ads with a high Quality Score pay far less than ads with a low Quality Score so make sure you're ads and landing page contain the same keywords you're targeting.

The Google Adwords platform allows you to select a maximum bid per click and a daily budget for your campaign. You can limit your risk. And once you set up your campaign, the ads show up within 15 minutes.

Sign up for an account. Give it a try, even if just for a week or two. It's fun and gets people to your website in a hurry!

Step-by-step action guide:

- ☐ *Get an account with Google Adwords.*
- ☐ *Walk through the set up process. It's easy.*
- ☐ *Write an ad to promote your business.*
- ☐ *Select keyword phrases to target.*
- ☐ *Use only 3 or 4-word keyword phrases.*
- ☐ *Select a maximum bid of 50¢ or 75¢.*
- ☐ *Set a daily budget of $10 and give it a try.*
- ☐ *Explore the Google Keyword Selector Tool.*
- ☐ *Ensure you have a high Quality Score.*
- ☐ *Targeted keywords = keywords in your ad.*
- ☐ *Targeted keywords = keywords on website.*
- ☐ *Play with the program and monitor results.*

Pay-Per-Click Advertising

57

Write a Press Release

Have you ever sent out a press release?

If you're like most small businesses, the answer is NO. But the opportunity with public relations and press releases is growing, not shrinking.

Back in the good old days, press releases were only intended for journalists and media coverage but the internet has changed that. Let's start the discussion by looking at today's marketing process.

Modern marketing can essentially be broken down into two stages. First, you have to market to people who do *not* yet know who you are. This is the process of finding, attracting and qualifying prospects. Second, once a prospect has found you, you have to market to them again, ensuring your company instills confidence with your audience.

What do people do when they hear about you or your company? Many of them look you up on Google or one of the other search engines. Maybe not all but many, and that percentage is growing every year.

Put your name or your company name into a Google search. What comes up? Anything? Good stuff? Bad stuff? Weird stuff?

When you send out a press release, you populate the internet with information that *you* control. That's a tremendous opportunity. There are platforms that allow you to distribute press releases to a huge number of news-related websites. One of my favorites is PRWeb.

http://www.prweb.com/

PRWeb has four primary distribution options ranging from $80 to $360 and they can put your news story on dozens of high-powered websites. So what does that mean? It means your news story will show up all over the first few pages of any Google search about you.

But the opportunity doesn't stop there. If you optimize your title and content with keywords, your story could come up for a whole bunch of other searches as well. That means you can use press releases to market to people who already know you *and* those who do not.

Here's the thing. Many of these news providers have big powerful websites. That means they rank high on the search engines. The trick is to leverage those high rankings by positioning keyword-optimized news stories about you and your company on those websites.

Done consistently, you can flood the internet with positive stories about you, your company and your keywords.

Of course, the traditional public relations strategies still offer opportunities and we should spend some time talking about press releases and how to write stories that get picked up by the traditional media outlets.

Chances are, your news story will never make the top headlines but that doesn't mean you won't get coverage. Think about the major news stories dominating the headlines today. Try to incorporate those headlines into your own story.

Media providers present the news in chunks. Watch your local news. You'll see for yourself. They almost always present three or four related stories at one time. The first one is usually the primary headline but two or three related stories often follow and that's what to shoot for.

Always think about what's going on in the world and try to piggy back on something the media outlets are already covering. There are lots of holidays during the year and weeks devoted towards one cause or another. These all represent opportunities for press releases.

Try to incorporate all three strategies in your press releases. Include your name or the name of your company. Optimize the title and story with keywords so the story gets found on search engines. Select an angle that incorporates a major news story or a special holiday to increase the odds that traditional media outlets pick it up.

Modern PR integrates all of these different considerations and offers a wide variety of benefits. Don't let those opportunities pass you by. Write a press release. Test it. See what happens. It will cost you $360 or less and might score you some valuable media publicity.

Step-by-step action guide:

- [ ] *Think about the big stories on the news.*
- [ ] *Incorporate those stories in press releases.*
- [ ] *Put your keywords in the title and content.*
- [ ] *Visit PRWeb and read about their services.*
- [ ] *Use a service to distribute your releases.*

Write a Press Release

58

Start a Group or Club

Can you be an effective group organizer?

You might surprise yourself. I did! Back in mid-2007, I stepped in as the organizer for an entrepreneur group on Meetup.com. The group had about 100 members at that time but they hadn't had a meeting in months and the group was falling apart.

At the time of this writing, my Meetup group has over 1000 members and is one of the 50 largest entrepreneur clubs in the country. It's called the Entrepreneur & Small Business Academy and we're now sponsored by American Express OPEN. Our membership is growing each month and I believe we're just getting started.

> http://www.meetup.com/academy/

The interesting thing is that I never invited a single member. They all found me! The Meetup platform hosts thousands of different groups and has millions of visitors each month. Many of those visitors are members of an existing group but they also browse through other groups that cater to their interests.

Meetup isn't the only platform that supports groups. Yahoo and Google both have platforms to organize groups. You can also start groups on MySpace, Facebook and LinkedIn among others. In each case, you can start a group and have people find you and join.

I like Meetup the best because I think the viral effect is the strongest on that platform. Right now, I'm getting one or two new members every single day!

The reality is that most Meetup groups don't do very well. Their meetings are poorly attended and their membership growth is anemic. Meanwhile, my group has one primary meeting each month and we usually get between 50 and 100 people in attendance.

I attribute the success of my group to three critical factors.

1. Content
2. Structure
3. Communication

Content. Whether your group is exclusively online or has an offline component, provide your membership with quality content. Give them good useful information. That's what they want. If you consistently deliver value, your group will grow.

Structure. Facilitate structured meetings. People like structure. They know exactly what to expect. Many leaders hate structure but followers love it. Obviously, the distinction between leaders and followers depends on the situation but the message is clear. Groups with structure do better than those without it.

Communication. Communication is critical. You need to keep your membership well informed about your activities as a group facilitator. Take a leadership role. Make decisions and tell your membership what's going on.

Meetup recently did a study and found that events with large descriptions (400 words or more) had better attendance than events with short descriptions. This is another angle to the communication element. Tell your members what to expect. They'll appreciate it.

You may or may not feel comfortable becoming a group organizer but the benefits are clear. Becoming an organizer has put me at the center of the entrepreneur community in the San Francisco Bay Area.

We have very productive meetings and most of our events are free. Our members receive clear value and that leaves me with tremendous social equity. People have done kind things for me and I count myself lucky to know such wonderful people.

I use Google Analytics to monitor my website statistics and my group homepage on Meetup consistently refers quality traffic to my Tactical Execution website. I get business from the group. I have found great resources in the group. I've made friends in the group. It's been a wonderful experience from the start.

Here's another angle. In June 2008, I bought a camcorder and started recording the presentations we have at our meetings. I post the videos on my YouTube channel, making the content available to a much broader audience.

http://www.youtube.com/tacticalexecution

The cool thing is that our meetings only take place once but the videos last forever! They become an annuity that I (and our speakers) benefit from long into the future. And besides that, it's fun!

I have already heard from two speakers who have secured new business with people who found them on my YouTube channel. That makes me feel great and it attracts other high-quality speakers to my group.

Meetup and YouTube make a great combination. It's changed my business and I hope it might one day change yours too.

There is tremendous demand among professionals for the information in this book and people are starting to form local networking groups on Meetup, covering a different chapter each week in local settings. You can find more information on the following website.

http://www.WebifyClub.com/

Organize your own local **Web**ify **Business Club** and we'll provide PDF agendas and worksheets to accompany each meeting. In other words, of Content, Structure and Communication, we'll provide the first two and Meetup will deliver members, putting you at the center of a productive business networking group in your community.

Step-by-step action guide:

☐ *Visit Meetup.com and search for keywords.*
☐ *See which groups exist and visit a few.*
☐ *Visit Yahoo Groups and Google Groups.*
☐ *Search groups on Facebook and LinkedIn.*
☐ *See what other groups are doing.*
☐ *Consider starting your own group or club.*
☐ *Content: deliver value to your members.*
☐ *Structure: facilitate well-organized events.*
☐ *Communication: keep members informed.*
☐ *Become known within your community.*
☐ *Visit the WebifyClub.com website.*
☐ *Consider organizing a local Webify group.*

Start a Group or Club

59

Wow Your Internet Audience

So ... how's your business doing?

We're approaching the finish line and we've covered a lot of different topics. Now, it's time to pull it all together. It's time to *wow* your internet audience. It's time to show them how solid your online identity has become.

The last major section of this book introduced different strategies you can use to drive traffic to your website. Hopefully, you've tried a few. If so, you have a number of profiles on the internet and little demonstrations of your expertise on a variety of different platforms.

Cross-reference everything!

If you published a few articles on EzineArticles, link to your "expert" author page. If you've been posting comments on popular online forums, link to your profile. If you uploaded some videos to YouTube, link to your channel. And if your press releases were picked up by major media websites, link to those stories.

Also, put links to your Twitter feed, your Facebook profile and your LinkedIn account. Post links to your profiles on social bookmarking platforms like DIGG, Delicious and StumbleUpon.

When people land on your website, you want them to be blown away with all the things you're doing online. You want emails that say "you're everywhere!" We've covered a lot in this book. Now, it's time to *wow* your audience with all your progress.

Of course, the final objective is to make money. That's what we're trying to do. At the beginning of the book, we spent some time defining your business model, organizing your content and packaging your value. Later, there was a chapter about writing effective sales copy for your products or services.

Now, the job shifts to one of calibration. Monitor your traffic and see where your website visitors are coming from. Check your Google Analytics regularly and see where people are coming from and where they're spending time on your website. Calibrate your activities to optimize results.

Here are the most common weak links:

1. low or inconsistent website traffic
2. low sign-up rates for intermediate content
3. low open rates on email subject lines
4. low conversion on email sales copy
5. website doesn't engage visitors or build trust
6. low conversion on website sales copy
7. products don't provide sufficient value

Measure each of these areas and commit to a process of continuous improvement. You can double your business by doubling your effectiveness of just *one* of these areas. If you double your effectiveness of *two*, your business could increase four-fold. If you double your effectiveness on *three*, your business could jump eight-fold.

Running a business in the internet age isn't rocket science. It's a process. And once you learn it, you can do it again and again. It all begins with demonstrating your expertise, providing value and building trust. After that, you invite your audience to review your advanced content and (hopefully) buy something.

By reading this book, you have become part of *my* business. As I mentioned in Chapter 41, I hope you will consider hiring me as a speaker or trainer, or passing my name along. That's *my* advanced content. That's what I want to do.

Tactical Execution > About > Speaking Engagements

I sincerely hope you can use this book as a guide to grow your business on the internet. Please keep me posted on your progress. Visit my website. Send me an email. Let me know how things are going. Tell me about your successes and your frustrations.

My goal is to package the best and most practical internet marketing training available anywhere. I can't do that unless I know how my suggestions deliver in real world situations. In that sense, my future success is in your hands and I'm excited to hear your stories.

Step-by-step action guide:

- ☐ *Make a list of all your online profiles.*
- ☐ *Wherever possible, link them all together.*
- ☐ *Show your audience what you have done.*
- ☐ *Always look for opportunities to integrate.*
- ☐ *Keep track of your successes and failures.*
- ☐ *Please keep me posted on your progress.*

Wow Your Internet Audience

60

Weekly Execution Plan

One of the most common reactions I get from people at my workshops is that they feel overwhelmed and don't know how to incorporate all my suggestions into their schedule.

As with any process, there are two aspects to a successful implementation. The first involves all the set-up work and the second involves the ongoing maintenance work that keeps the strategy engaged.

Many of the suggestions in this book involve some set-up work and the only way to get that stuff done is to allocate the necessary time and plow through it. But the ongoing tasks can eventually be done with efficiency.

The following is one possible weekly task schedule and as you can see, it requires less than 90 minutes each day. Is it too simplistic? Absolutely not. This basic execution plan, done consistently, would yield a powerful and impressive internet marketing presence.

I have included time estimates for each task. Obviously, it will take you longer the very first time you do it. But after some practice, you'll be familiar with the steps and the time required will drop significantly.

Monday Morning   Minutes

☐	*Record an Utter with cell phone.*	2
☐	*Post an ad on Craigslist.*	5
☐	*Check your blog subscriptions.*	25

Monday Afternoon   Minutes

☐	*Tweet about something.*	2
☐	*Write a 500+ word blog post.*	45
☐	*Submit it to bookmarking sites.*	10

Tuesday Morning   Minutes

☐	*Record an Utter with cell phone.*	2
☐	*Be active on social networks.*	15
☐	*Post five comments on a forum.*	30

Tuesday Afternoon   Minutes

☐	*Tweet about something.*	2
☐	*Submit your post to carnivals.*	25
☐	*Check your Google Analytics.*	15

Wednesday Morning   Minutes

☐	*Record an Utter with cell phone.*	2
☐	*Post an ad on Craigslist.*	5
☐	*Work on a press release.*	45

Wednesday Afternoon   Minutes

- [ ] *Tweet about something.*   2
- [ ] *Modify your blog post slightly.*   25
- [ ] *Publish it on article directories.*   10

Thursday Morning   Minutes

- [ ] *Record an Utter with cell phone.*   2
- [ ] *Be active on social networks.*   15
- [ ] *Post five comments on a forum.*   30

Thursday Afternoon   Minutes

- [ ] *Tweet about something.*   2
- [ ] *Make your post into an ebook.*   30
- [ ] *Upload it to an ebook directory.*   10

Friday Morning   Minutes

- [ ] *Record an Utter with cell phone.*   2
- [ ] *Post an ad on Craigslist.*   5
- [ ] *Improve your site in some way.*   30

Friday Afternoon   Minutes

- [ ] *Tweet about something.*   2
- [ ] *Record a video about your post.*   50
- [ ] *Upload the video to YouTube.*   5

Discipline and consistency define success. It's just like
going to the gym. The place is packed in January and
empty by March. All the New Year's Resolution people get
excited for a month or two, but disappear thereafter.

Those who win are those who stick with it. The suggested
weekly execution plan on the previous two pages is simple
but powerful. It doesn't take *that* much time but can
deliver impressive results if followed consistently.

As I mentioned at the beginning of this chapter, the set up
work takes time. No question. If this is all new to you,
there's a bunch of infrastructure to build. Profiles.
Accounts. Friends. Connections. Integration. But once
that stuff is done, it gets a lot easier.

I hope you give these strategies a try. The internet has
completely changed my business – all for the better – and
it can change yours too. You'll find parallel worlds you've
never seen and opportunities you never noticed. You'll find
old friends from high school and make new ones all across
the globe.

Allocate the time to work through the set up requirements.
Commit to building the foundation. After that, find a way
to incorporate the strategies we've covered into your daily
routine and let the internet revolution propel your business
(and your life) forward.

Good luck! And please keep me posted.

*Thank you for reading this book. If you found it useful,
please tell your friends about it. Your endorsement is
worth far more than my own marketing efforts. Also, if you
have success with these strategies, let me know. I may
include your story in a press release (at my cost) which
could result in valuable publicity for both of us.*